CRAFT IT!

CRAFT IT!

50 Fun Stamp, Paper & Polymer Clay Projects

JOE RHATIGAN, RAIN NEWCOMB
& IRENE SEMANCHUK DEAN

BARNES & NOBLE BOOKS

NEW YORK

Library of Congress Cataloging-in-Publication Data Available

2   4   6   8   10   9   7   5   3   1

Published by Sterling Publishing Co., Inc.
387 Park Avenue South, New York, NY 10016
© 2005 by Sterling Publishing Co., Inc.
This book comprises material from the following Sterling Publishing Co., Inc. titles:
Kids' Crafts: Stamp It! © 2004 by Lark Books
Kids' Crafts: Paper Fantastic © 2004 by Lark Books
Kids' Crafts: Polymer Clay © 2003 by Irene Semanchuk Dean

Design by StarGraphics Studio

Printed in China
All rights reserved

ISBN 0-7607-9514-2

Table of contents

Introduction

With *Craft It!: 50 Fun Stamp, Paper & Polymer Clay Projects*, you will fold, cut, roll, mold, and squish to your heart's content. These amazing and easy projects are perfect for rainy days or those days when your artistic soul calls. You can do these great projects by yourself or invite friends over and have a crafting party.

In the first section, "Super Stamp Crafts," you will learn how to transform a boring pair of sneakers or an old bandanna into something awesome that stands out from the crowd. Just take your own handmade or store-bought stamp, or a found object such as a potato masher, apply some ink or paint to it, and print the image onto paper, fabric, wood, or almost anything you like. You will be able to give the ordinary, ranging from lamp shades to book covers to picture frames, your personalized touch. These stamp projects are fun, innovative, and super-cool! You will want to stamp everything.

The second part, "Awesome Paper Creations," will change how you look at paper. No longer will paper be something you do your homework on, but rather you will see it as an art form. The fantastic paper projects in *Craft It!* are so easy and so much fun. You can jazz up your favorite journal or make an amazing silhouette of your most beloved pet or even decorate your Christmas tree with these clever projects. You can decorate your room with the Garland, or you can wear the Book Necklace and the Interlocking Paper Bracelet. Spice up the dinner table with the Place Mat and the Paper Bouquet. Or make your own gift wrap. The possibilities are endless.

The third section, "Fabulous Polymer Clay Objects," gets a little messy but is certainly no less fun. Polymer clay is one of the most bendable, flexible, and colorful materials you will ever work with. Not only is it inexpensive, but you can also bake it in a kitchen oven. Best of all, there's almost no limit to what you can create. Make a set of Novel Knobs for your dresser or a Space Mobile to hang from your ceiling. Create a set of Pushpinzzzzzzzz for the coolest bulletin board ever.

Whatever you choose, the polymer clay projects are colorful, unique, and totally awesome. Use your imagination!

All the materials you will need to get started are available either around the house or at your local craft store. But often the most extraordinary creations come from the most ordinary materials. So do not be afraid to try out ideas and test new, unusual materials.

The terrific projects in *Craft It!* present stamping, paper, and polymer clay crafts in a cool, entertaining way, meant to encourage you to experiment, to imagine, and to develop your personal artistic expression, all at the same time. Feel free to express yourself and make the projects your own by changing colors, patterns, or shapes. Anyone can be an artist—the projects in this book just help you get started!

Super Stamp Crafts

Stamping Madness in one Easy Lesson

TRUE OR FALSE?

Circle the correct answer.

T F With a little piece of rubber or foam and some paint you can transform a boring pair of sneakers into something glamorous and cool.

T F Little old you can take some leaves and other stuff from nature and turn a plain canvas bag into an awesome fashion statement.

T F All that's standing between you and a fabulously decorated book cover is a piece of bubble wrap, some paint, and a paper bag.

If you answered "True" to all the above questions, **congratulations**, this chapter is for you.

You realize that the wonderfully mad world of stamping is a limitless opportunity to create fun, beautiful, stunning, funny, and engrossing projects, gifts, and decorations.

If you answered "False" to all the above questions, **congratulations**, this chapter is for you. You are about to realize that the wonderfully mad world of stamping is a limitless opportunity to… Well, you get what we mean.

Whether you know about stamping or not, this chapter is chock full of project ideas, techniques, information, and more for kids who want to decorate, create, and play around with stamps. The great thing about stamping is that you don't need to know much to get started. You also don't need to buy much. Questions?

What is stamping, anyway?

Stamping is taking a rubber, foam, homemade, or found object, applying some ink or paint to it, and printing the image, shape, or design onto cards, socks, dog bowls, jackets, picture frames, or just about anything else you can think of.

What do I need to get started?

A couple of stamps, something to stamp on, some ink, and this book.

Is stamping addictive?

Highly.

What's in the chapter?

Fourteen creative projects with step-by-step instructions, a bunch of ways for you to make your own stamps, and everything you need to know to get started.

When can I get started?

Right away. So, what are you waiting for? Class dismissed. Turn the page!

Getting Started

Whether you're brand new to stamping or you consider yourself an old pro, read this section before jumping into the projects. We'll fill you in on what you need and how to stamp.

Rubber stamps are the most popular type of store-bought stamp. They're easy to use and, with proper care, will last a long time.

THE STAMPS

Once you start stamping, you may never stop. It's fun buying rubber or foam stamps, and it's even more fun making your own. Here is just a sampling of the stamps you can use for the projects in this chapter.

Store-Bought Stamps

You can buy rubber or foam stamps in all shapes and sizes, though foam stamps tend to be less intricate in their design.

Foam stamps usually have bold designs on them.

Homemade Stamps

Sometimes the one stamp you're looking for just doesn't exist. Luckily, making your own stamps is easy. You can make stamps out of cardboard, string, meat trays, erasers, and more. Instructions for several versions appear through-out this book.

A small selection of homemade stamps that appear throughout this book.

You can make stamps out of fruit. Potato carving is an old favorite. See page 30.

The three most important things to remember when making your own stamps

1 When you're carving a stamp, the areas that stick up will be the colored-in areas.

2 Go slow. You can always carve more material off, but you can't put it back on.

3 Your stamp will be the reverse of the image you carve. If you want to stamp a word or num-ber, !DRAWKCAB TI ETIRW.

Found Stamps

Sponges, potato mashers, bubble wrap, body parts, and more can be used as stamps. It won't be long before you're finding lots of fun things you never thought could be used as stamps.

If it's got a neat outline, texture, or if it's just plain cool, stamp it! Clockwise from left: shoe, computer parts, mesh, shelf liner, bubble wrap, and more mesh.

Sponges are great for stamping backgrounds.

What other objects can you find in nature to use as stamps?

INKS AND PAINTS

What kind of ink or paint you use to stamp with depends on what you're stamping on.

Dye-based inks are thin, water-based inks that are available in pads or markers. (The markers are called printing pens or brush markers.) Use these inks with detailed stamps. These inks dry quickly, although they tend to bleed on paper and fade over time.

Also available in pads or markers, pigment inks are thicker and are made so that they won't bleed with other colors on paper. It takes a longer time for these inks to dry, and they won't dry at all on glossy paper. Pigment inks tend not to fade.

You can use acrylic paints to stamp on wood and other materials.

Crafter's ink is good for wood, fabric, shrink plastic, and metal.

You can get any kind of ink in a pad made especially for stamping.

Fabric paints can be used for stamping on fabric. Read the instructions on the containers before using. You can also find fabric ink pads and markers in craft stores.

Printing pens work just like markers.

PAPER

Paper isn't just the white stuff you print your homework out on. There are tons of different kinds of paper in all sorts of different colors, designs, sizes, shapes, and textures, and they all absorb ink a little differently. Here are some of the common types of paper.

Card Stock

This is the most versatile paper. It's smooth and has a fairly heavy weight, which means it's thicker and stiffer than the pages of this book. It comes in all sorts of colors and patterns, and you can get it in a matte (not shiny) or glossy finish (very shiny). If you use pigment inks on glossy card stock, you'll have to heat-emboss the stamped image in order to set the ink (see page 47). The ink won't sink into the paper otherwise.

Text Weight

This paper is a lot like computer paper. If you don't want to decorate the background of your project, you can find this paper in any color and with a whole variety of patterns already on it.

Tissue Paper

Tissue paper is fun to stamp on. It's very fragile, so you'll have to be gentle with it. Dye-based inks work best on tissue paper.

Vellum

This smooth, see-through paper comes in text weight and card stock. It's glossy, so you're better off using dye-based inks or using the heat-embossing technique on page 47.

OTHER MATERIALS AND TOOLS

You've got your stamps. You've got your inks and paints. Now what? Here are the rest of the tools and materials you need to get yourself going.

You never know when you're going to want to draw a temporary line on your project to keep everything lined up. Keep a pencil and ruler on hand so that you're ready to make that line anytime. A ruler is handy for when you want to stamp in grids or patterns. Draw guiding lines onto your project lightly in pencil. After you've stamped everything (and let the ink dry), go back and erase the lines. And, of course, you can't live without scissors.

Also, cover your work surface with newspaper. Not only will it keep the table clean, but you'll also be able to test your stamps on it. You should also stamp on top of a stack of scrap paper or newspaper. The paper creates a very nice padding to press the stamps into as you print them. (This makes your stamped images show up better.) Use paper towels for cleaning up your stamps. Wet ink is a lot easier to clean up than dry ink, so keep those paper towels within reach.

INKING THE STAMP

Depending on what kind of ink you're using, you'll use different methods to get the ink onto the stamp.

Using Ink Pads

1 If you're working with a stamp pad, press the stamp into the pad gently. You have to be careful not to get too much ink on your stamp, so just set the stamp on the ink pad and tap the back of it gently. (Sometimes it works better to press the pad onto the stamp.)

2 Test the stamp on a piece of newspaper to see how well you inked the image. You can usually stamp several times before re-inking.

A brayer is a handheld roller that you can use to ink stamps or create backgrounds.

Using a Foam Paintbrush

1 Pour some of the paint onto wax paper or a paper plate.

2 Dab the brush in the paint and brush it onto the stamp. This technique may require some practice as you figure out just how much (or how little) paint you need. Do lots of test stamps on newspaper.

Using Pens

1 If you're using the printing pens to ink your stamps, simply place your stamp right side up in front of you and start coloring.

2 Apply the lighter colored markers first and work your way to the darkest. That way you won't contaminate your colors.

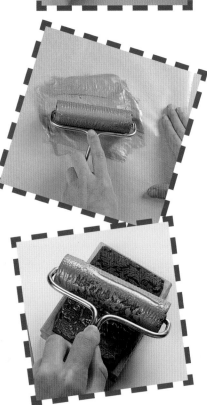

Using a Brayer

1 Pour some ink onto a smooth, flat surface, such as a piece of wax paper or a paper plate.

2 Roll the brayer back and forth over the ink or paint until it gets tacky.

3 Roll the brayer across the surface of the stamp.

COLORING STAMPS

Coloring stamps with printing pens is a great way to add flair to your images. It works really well on foam stamps that don't have too much detail. If you use these techniques on highly detailed stamps, remember that you need to color in only the raised areas.

Coloring Stamps with Different Sections

A lot of foam stamps have different sections already separated and ready to color in. To work with these stamps, simply use the printing pens to color in the different sections of the stamp.

Rainbow Stamps

To give your image a rainbow look when you stamp it, select several different colors of printing pens. Put them in the order you want to use them and start coloring at one edge of the stamp with the lightest color. Then color another section with a darker color. Make sure to work from lightest to darkest so that the colors don't mix and get muddy. Don't worry if the edges are mixing where the colors meet. This will add to the rainbow effect. When you're finished coloring, stamp.

Making Patterns on Stamps

You can also use printing pens to make a pattern on your stamp. Decide what kind of pattern you want. Then, start to color the stamp with the lightest-color marker you'll use. Work your way up to the darkest color. You'll get better at this step the more you do it, so don't freak out if you don't do it perfectly the first time.

Special Tip

If it takes you a really long time to color in your stamp, breathe on it before stamping it. This will remoisten any ink that might have dried.

STAMPING ON PAPER, FABRIC, WOOD, OR WHATEVER

Four Easy Steps to Success

1 If you're stamping on paper, set the paper on several pieces of scrap paper or newspaper. Ink the stamp.

2 Gently set the inked stamp on your paper. Be careful not to wiggle it or move it around at all after you've set it down. The image will blur if you do.

3 Press the back of the stamp evenly with your hands or fingertips. Make sure you get the center and all of the edges.

4 Carefully lift the stamp straight up and off the paper. Set it aside and look at the stamped image.

Troubleshooting

If the whole image on the stamp didn't print, try it again. Make sure the stamp is fully inked. You may want to put it on a different part of the ink pad just in case part of the pad has gone dry.

When you stamp the image, make sure that you're applying the same amount of pressure over the whole stamp.

If the image didn't print clearly or the details of the stamp were blurry, you might have too much ink on your stamp. Clean off the ink with a paper towel and try it again. Be gentler when you press the stamp into the ink pad, or try using the brayer to ink the stamp. If you're still having trouble, try it with thinner ink.

If the image is blurry and smeared, you probably got a little too jumpy when you were placing it on the paper. Be very careful not to bump, shake, or wiggle at all when you're stamping the image. Don't rock it back and forth either. One of the best ways to get a blurry image is to put your stamp where you think you want it and then decide that it should actually be just a little bit to the right (or the left, or wherever). Don't try even the teeniest adjustment on the stamp after it has made contact with the paper. Instead, use the pencil and the ruler to make light placement guides *before* you start stamping.

More Thoughts on Stamping

When stamping on wood, follow the instructions for stamping on paper, but make sure to use pigment ink pads or acrylic paints.

When stamping on fabric, put a piece of cardboard on your work surface or inside a shirt, sock, or pillowcase before stamping. This will keep any ink or paint from seeping through the front side and onto the back. Also, make sure you're using fabric ink, and have an adult help you set the dye so you can wash the project.

When stamping on metal, use metal paint.

FUN WAYS TO DECORATE YOUR STAMPED IMAGES

Just because you stamped a bunch of images on a project doesn't mean you have to be finished.

Chalks

Colored chalks have a light look sort of like watercolors. They're not always easy to control in small, tight areas.

First, stamp the image with a dark ink and let it dry. Then make small circles of color with the chalk. Use your fingers to smear the color around. Don't forget to wash your fingers off before using another color. If you're using more than one color, make sure to start with the lighter colors and work your way to the darker colors. After you've colored in your stamp completely, spray the image with a matte-finish sealer to keep the chalk from rubbing off.

Colored Pencils

Colored pencils are great for coloring in stamps.

First, stamp the image with a dark ink and let it dry. Then, color it in with the colored pencils. Cross-hatching is a fun technique for this. Color in one direction and then work in the opposite direction. If you feel like having a little color adventure, use a different color when you scribble in the opposite direction. Sharp points work best for filling in small areas, and dull points are great for covering larger areas with a softer shade of color. You can also use crayons, of course.

Markers

You can use regular markers or printing pens to color in your stamped images. This technique gives you the boldest, brightest colors.

First, stamp the image with a dark ink and let it dry. Then color it in with the markers. If your markers have two different ends, a skinny one and fat one, use the skinny end to color in the details and the small areas and the fat end to color in the bigger areas. Work from your lightest color to your darkest to avoid having the colors mix together and get muddy looking. Be careful not to go over the same spot too many times. The color will get really dark and you'll be able to see the brush marks. The color might also run if you put too much on.

Watercolor Paints

Watercolor paints will give your stamps a soft, artistic look. And because you're being artistic, don't be too concerned about staying in the lines!

First, stamp the image with a dark ink and let it dry. Wet the paintbrush and make tiny circles with it in the first color you want to use. Test the color on a piece of scrap paper to see if it's too light or too dark. If it's too dark, add more water. If it's too light, dab some of the water out of the paint with a clean paper towel and try it again. When you've got the color you want, start painting. Use a thin brush for painting in the smaller areas.

Restamping

Sometimes one stamp just isn't enough. You can do some really interesting things by stamping over the same stamp with a different color. Stamp your first image, clean off the stamp, and wait for the ink to dry completely. Then re-ink the stamp with a different color and place it over the first stamp. Don't worry too much about getting the stamp lined up in exactly the same place as before—not only is it impossible, but it also won't look nearly as cool.

CLEANING UP

What!? Stamping is supposed to be fun, and cleaning up doesn't sound like fun. Well, maybe it's not, but cleaning up your stamps and workspace immediately after you finish a project will make it a lot more fun to return to your stamping later.

Cleaning Your Stamps

As tempting as it might be to submerge your inky stamps in a sink full of sudsy water, don't. The water will make the glue that holds the stamp to the handle come apart. If you immediately wipe off your stamps with a damp paper towel, you shouldn't have too much trouble keeping them squeaky clean. If you do run into

trouble, use an old toothbrush to scrub the ink off the stamp's surface. If that doesn't work, dilute window cleaner with some water and use that to clean up the ink. Permanent inks have to be removed with a special cleaning solution.

Putting It All Away

After you've washed every speck of ink (more or less) off your stamps, dry them with an old towel. Gather all of your ink pads and markers. Make sure ink pad lids and printing pen caps are tightly closed.

Put all of your stamps, inks, papers, scissors, and other supplies in a big cardboard box. Store your papers flat, ink pads upside down, and stamps clean, dry, and image-side down. Now you have a portable studio. Decorate the box with, of course, stamped designs! Now, when inspiration hits, all you have to do is pull out the box and start stamping.

The Projects

Now, without further delay, without a single solitary word to the wise, with no more fooling around, here they are: the wonderful, fantastic projects...plus, a few final words.

You can choose from the projects here, including several ways to make your own stamps. Start small and easy and work your way up to the projects that may seem challenging.

Also, you can do these projects exactly as they appear in the chapter (you can even purchase the same stamps used in the projects) or branch out on your own. Take a project and run with it. Work with the stamps you like or have. Let your imagination go wild. It's up to you how you approach these projects, as long as you get an adult to help you when necessary. With some practice and patience you'll find that even if you thought your dog had more artistic talent than you did, your projects will look pretty cool. See if your dog can top that. All that really matters is that you enjoy yourself. Okay, we mean it now. No more words. We're done. Now it's your turn.

DIVE ON IN!

Starlight Gift Wrap

You can create a card or a gift tag with the same stamp you use on the gift wrap.

What You Need

Snowflake star stamp
White ink pad
Tissue paper
Pencil with unused eraser

What You Do

1 Choose the color tissue paper that you want to use. Lay the paper flat on your work surface. Put a scrap piece of tissue paper behind it since the stamp ink may go through the first layer and onto the table you're working on.

2 Stamp the star randomly over the paper with white ink, rotating the stamp as you go to add some variety.

3 Ink the pencil eraser. (It's now a stamp!) Use it to fill in between the stars.

4 Let the ink dry before using the wrapping paper. When wrapping the present, add another sheet of plain unstamped tissue paper behind the stamped paper. The tissue paper is see-through, and adding another sheet will make it easier to see the stamps and not get a peek at what's inside.

Giant Duffel Bag

- - - - - - - - - - - - - - - - - - -

This bag is great for sleepovers and vacations (plus, it'll hold all the dirty clothes from your bedroom floor).

What You Need

Flower-shaped cookie cutter
Flower-shaped eraser
Assorted foam stamps
Fabric paint ink pads in assorted colors
1 yard of fabric or large pillowcase
Matching thread
Sewing machine
Iron and ironing board
2 yards of ribbon, 1 inch wide
Scissors
Large safety pin
Cardboard
Paper towel

What You Do

1 If you don't want to do any major sewing, simply use a big pillowcase, cut a hole in the "tunnel" around the opening of the pillowcase, and skip to step 6.

2 Wash and dry the fabric. If you don't know how to sew, get an adult to help you. Fold the fabric, right sides together, and sew down the long seam and across one of the shorter seams. Leave the other side open. You now have what looks like a big pillowcase, inside out.

3 Have an adult help you press the seams open with the iron. Press down the top raw edge 2 inches to create a hem. Press the raw edge of opening under ½ inch. Then fold it over again, making a 2-inch overlap.

4 Sew the hem in place, leaving a 6-inch opening in the seam to thread the ribbon through.

5 Stitch a buttonhole on the outside of the bag in the hem, or simply cut a ½-inch-wide opening to stick the ribbon ends through.

7 Sew the 6-inch opening shut. Be careful not to sew into the ribbon. Turn the duffel bag right side out and iron it.

8 Cut a piece of cardboard and place it inside the duffel bag. Stamp the front side of the bag and let it dry.

9 Stamp the other side of the bag and let it dry.

10 Put a paper towel over the stamped areas and have an adult help you iron over it to set the paint. Another way to set the fabric is to throw it in the dryer on medium heat for 30 minutes.

6 Pin the safety pin to one end of the ribbon. Thread it all the way around the inside of the hem or tunnel. Pull both ends of the ribbon through the button-hole or cut in the hem. Stitch the ends of the ribbon together.

Sunny citrus Picture frame

Leave a good impression with this cool stamping technique.

What You Need

1 orange
2 lemon halves
Lime green, orange, lemon yellow, and tangerine acrylic paints
Paintbrush
Wooden picture frame
Kitchen cutting board
Kitchen knife*
Paring knife*
Spoon
Paper towels
Wax paper
Foam paintbrush
Scrap paper
Fine-tip paintbrush

*Ask an adult to help you cut and prepare the fruit.

What You Do

1 Paint the frame with the lime green paint. Let it dry.

2 Place the orange on top of the kitchen cutting board. Use the kitchen knife to cut the orange in half, horizontally slicing through the middle of the fruit.

5 While the orange dries, repeat steps 2 through 4 with two lemons.

3 Use the paring knife to cut the flesh out of one half of the orange, while leaving the raised divisions intact. Carefully scoop out the fruit with the spoon.

4 Once the flesh is removed from all sections, drain the remaining juice from the orange half onto a paper towel. Repeat with the other half, then allow the orange halves to air-dry for about 30 minutes.

6 Pour some orange acrylic paint onto the wax paper. Use the foam paintbrush to paint the orange, then stamp it onto a piece of scrap paper. If your stamp is too heavy, press the fruit

on the paper again without applying additional paint. Use the fine-tip paintbrush to fill in any orange skin sections that aren't taking paint. Repeat this testing process until you're happy with the results.

7 Stamp the orange onto your frame. Vary the placement of the orange stamps on your frame, and even let a few trail off the edges. Let the paint dry.

8 Repeat using the yellow paint and one lemon half. Repeat again with the second lemon half and the tangerine paint.

Fruits and Veggies

Even if you don't like the way mushrooms taste, you might like the way they look—especially after you turn them into stamps. Making stamps out of fruits and vegetables is a great way to create unique designs.

Mushroom Stamps

1 Cut a mushroom in half and dab the flat side with a paper towel. This will get rid of any excess moisture and give you a clean, dry surface to ink.

2 Ink the mushroom with an ink pad, foam paintbrush, or brayer and stamp it.

3 Don't eat the inked mushroom!

Other Fruits and Veggies

You can use this technique with just about any fruit or vegetable. Try stamping with a pear or apple. You probably can't stamp with a tomato or any other really, really wet fruit or veggie because the ink won't stick to it. If you work up an appetite while stamping, remember to eat ink-free fruits and veggies—not your stamping supplies.

The Famous Potato Stamp

Perhaps the most famous of all vegetable stamps is the potato stamp.

1 Make sure you have adult supervision when making a potato stamp. To make your first potato stamp, start out using a cookie cutter that will fit inside the potato as a guide.

2 Slice the potato in half lengthwise and press the cookie cutter into it.

3 Slice around the cookie cutter with a kitchen knife and remove all the flesh outside the image.

4 Make sure the image that you'll be stamping sticks up at least ¼ inch so that the ink will go only on the image and not the background.

5 Ink the potato and stamp it.

6 When you're ready to create your own designs in the potato, slice it in half and draw your design onto it with a felt-tipped marker.

7 Then carve away the excess potato. (Remember, carve away the part that you don't want to be inked.)

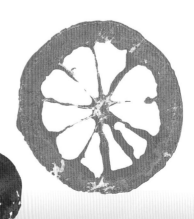

Hand Towel

Hands down, this is the most awesome towel ever.

What You Need

A hand (or two)
Assorted colors of nontoxic fabric paints
Terry cloth or fine-weave cotton hand towel, prewashed and dried
Cardboard
Wax paper
Foam paintbrush
Small paintbrush (optional)
Paper towels
Iron or use of a clothes dryer

What You Do

1 Lay the towel flat on top of a piece of cardboard.

2 Place some paint onto the wax paper. If you're using a brightly colored towel, be sure to use bright paints in contrasting colors that will show up well. Use the foam paintbrush to paint onto the surface of one hand.

3 Press that hand firmly onto the surface of the towel. (Practice on some newspaper first.)

4 Slowly lift your hand off of the towel as you would a stamp.

5 Do it again. If you're switching to another color, wash the hand before repeating. Vary the direction of the handprint for an energized, fun look. Repeat the direction of the print in order to create a graphic pattern.

6 If more definition is needed on some of the prints, use the paintbrush to add paint where needed.

7 Either place some paper towels over the dry handprints and have an adult help you iron over them, or place the towel in the dryer on medium heat for 30 minutes.

Simply Divine Sneakers

These shoes have the best of both worlds: they're comfortable AND glamorous.

What You Need

Shoe stamp
Fabric ink pad and pen in colors of your choice
Canvas tennis shoes
Newspaper

What You Do

1 Stuff the shoes with newspaper and remove the shoelaces. Make sure the paper is in there snugly so the sneakers are firm enough to stamp on.

2 Ink the shoe stamp. Make sure you get plenty of ink on it.

3 Stamp the shoe. Stamp it again. And again. And again. Do this for as long as you want. Color in some of the stamped images with fabric ink pens if you want.

Dog Bowl and Mat

Hey, even dogs deserve to dine in style.

What You Need

Knife, fork, spoon, dog, bone,
 and fire hydrant stamps
Red metal paint
Red, black, and silver fabric paint
Scissors
Piece of heavy canvas or foam
Foam paintbrush
Metal dog bowl
Silver glitter fabric paint
Paintbrush
Acrylic spray sealer

What You Do

1 Cut a bone shape out of the canvas or foam. Set it aside.

2 Apply the red metal paint to the bone stamp with the foam brush and stamp it around the edge of the dog bowl. Let it dry.

3 Put the dog bowl in the center of the canvas and stamp the knife, fork, and spoon around it. Stamp the dog, bone, and fire hydrant on the canvas. Use the silver glitter fabric paint to accent the fork, knife, and spoon images.

4 Once the mat is dry, spray it with the sealer.

Sun Card

Need a little sunshine in your life? This card will make the sun pop right out.

What You Need

Sun-shaped stamp
Black ink pad
Dark blue, white, and orange card stock
Pencil and ruler
Craft chalks or colored pencils
Scissors
Glue stick
Rhinestones with flat backs
1/8-inch hole punch
Cutting mat or cardboard
Craft knife
Bone folder or ballpoint pen that's out of ink

What You Do

1 Cut a 4¼ x 11-inch piece of dark blue card stock. Fold it in half to make the outer card, and set it aside.

2 Cut a 4⅛ x 10½-inch piece of white card stock. This will be the pop-up part of your card. With the pencil and ruler, lightly draw a line vertically across the middle of the card stock.

3 Ink the rubber stamp with black ink and stamp it in the center of the white card stock.

4 Stamp the image again on another piece of white card stock.

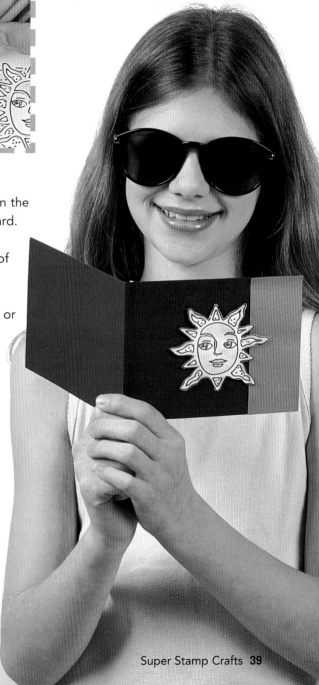

5 Color the suns with the chalks or colored pencils. See page 20 for more information on working with chalks and colored pencils. Cut out the second sun you stamped. This sun is for the front of the card.

6 Glue small rhinestones to the design and use a small hole punch. Don't cut, punch, or add rhinestones to that middle line you drew in step 2.

7 Place the sun design on the cutting mat or cardboard. Use the craft knife to cut along the top and bottom of the whole image (including any other decorations you drew). Don't cut on the left or right side of the image.

Sun card

8 If you want, make additional decorative cuts in and around the stamp. For example, you can cut out paper inside the sun's rays.

9 Put the ruler on the pencil line you drew in step 2. Use the bone folder or ballpoint pen to score along the pencil line above and below the stamped

image. Reposition the ruler along the left edge of the image and score it again. Do the same on the right side of the image.

10 Fold the card stock along the scored line in the center, carefully pulling the stamped image toward you as you fold. The creases above and below the image make a "valley" or V fold.

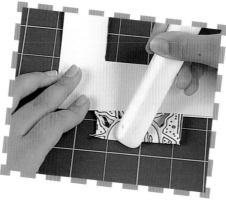

The stamped image itself will have a "mountain" fold, while the score lines along either side will become "valleys." Once the card stock is folded correctly, rub the bone folder along the outside of the card stock to crease the folds.

11 Glue the pop-up to the inside of the dark blue outer card. Erase the pencil line.

12 Glue the sun that you colored and cut out earlier to the front of the card with a strip of orange card stock (see photo on page 39 for placement).

Bookmark

Hey, stop folding down the pages in your books. It's easy to create a bookmark.

What You Need

Shoe, purse, and hat rubber
    stamps
Black ink pad
White card stock
Scissors, ruler, and pencil
Purple, magenta, and pink paint
Wax paper
Foam paintbrush
Hole punch
Tassel

What You Do

1 Cut the card stock to the size you want for the bookmark.

2 Pour a little bit of each color of paint onto the wax paper.

3 Dip the flat end of the foam brush into the paint and use it to decorate the card stock. Let the paint dry before adding a new color.

4 Flip the card stock over and paint the other side.

5 Once the bookmark is dry, stamp the shoe, purse, and hat stamps onto both sides of the card stock.

6 If you want, bring the finished bookmark to a copy center and have it laminated. Then punch a hole in the top and attach the tassel.

Too Cool Bandannas

Fashionable, fun, and easy to make!

YOUR-NAME-HERE SCARF

What You Need

Name stamp
Black fabric paint
Bandanna
Plastic jewels
Small paintbrush
Glue

What You Do

1 Place a piece of cardboard on your work surface, and place the bandanna face up on top of it.

2 Stamp your name onto the bandanna with the black fabric paint. Let it dry.

3 Put a paper towel over the stamped areas of the bandanna and have an adult help you iron over it to set the paint. Another way to set the fabric is to throw it in the dryer on medium heat for 30 minutes.

4 After the paint has been set, decorate the bandanna with the plastic jewels. Brush glue onto the back of each jewel and press it into place.

What You Need To Make A Name Stamp

Your favorite stamp-making technique
Scrap paper
Tracing paper
Pencil

What You Do

1 Pick your favorite stamp-making technique.

2 Write your name in cool letters on a piece of scrap paper. Trace over the letters with the tracing paper and pencil.

3 Flip the tracing paper upside down on the stamp-making material and rub the back of it to transfer your design.

LIP SCARF

What You Need

Lip stamp
Red and pink fabric paint
Scrap cardboard
Pink bandanna
Paper towel
Iron or use of a clothes dryer
Small paintbrush
Red glitter glue

What You Do

1 Follow the instructions for the previous scarf, but use the lip stamp and the red and pink fabric paint.

2 After the paint has been set, use the small paintbrush to highlight the lips with the red glitter glue.

Flower Power cards

Here are just three examples of the thousands of beautiful and professional-looking cards you can create with stamps.

What You Need

Flower, letter, and grass stamps
Purple and green printing pens
White, green, and red ink pads
Orange card and envelope
Clear embossing powder and
   heat gun (optional)
Craft knife (get an adult's help)

What You Do

1 Unfold the card and lay it flat in front of you. Color in the flower stamp with the purple and green printing pens. Stamp it so the top of the flower is above the fold line.

2 With an adult's supervision, heat-emboss the stamped image (see page 47) if you want.

GREEN CARD

3 Ink the letter stamps with the white ink and stamp the name of the person the card is for below the flower. Heat-emboss the letters.

4 Ink the grass stamp with the green ink pad, stamp it along the bottom of the card, and emboss the images.

5 Ink the small flower stamp with the red ink pad and stamp it randomly across the background of the card.

6 With the craft knife, carefully cut around the part of the main flower stamp that is above the folded line. Refold the card so that the top of the flower sticks up.

What You Need

Flower stamp
Black ink pad
Green card and envelope
Copper embossing powder
   and heat gun (optional)
Scissors

What You Do

1 Ink the flower stamp and stamp it once along the bottom edge of the card.

2 With an adult's supervision, heat-emboss the stamped image if you want (see page 47 to learn how to heat-emboss).

3 Stamp and emboss more flowers the way you just did. Remember to stamp one on the flap of the envelope.

4 Use the scissors to cut away some of the paper around the bottom edge of the flowers. Follow the lines of the embossed images.

flower Power cards

YELLOW CARD

What You Need

Flower and grass stamps
Purple and green printing pens
White card stock
Clear embossing powder and
  heat gun (optional)
Scissors
Yellow card and envelope
Craft knife (get an adult's help)
Glue

What You Do

1 Ink the flower stamp with the purple printing pen. Stamp it onto the white card stock once.

2 With an adult's supervision, heat-emboss the image (see page 47) if you want.

3 Repeat steps 1 and 2 until you have stamped and embossed six flowers. Cut out all of the flowers.

4 Arrange five of the flowers on the front of the yellow card. Trace around three of them with the green printing pen. Unfold the card and cut out the area inside of the green line with the craft knife.

5 Position three flowers inside of the card so that they'll show through the windows you just cut out. Make the windows bigger if you need to, then run the green printing pen along the edge. Glue the flowers into place on the inside and outside of the card.

6 Glue the last flower to the outside of the envelope. Ink the grass stamp with the green printing pen and stamp it along the borders.

Heat Embossing

With this technique, you can create raised and shiny stamped images. It's simple and fun, and the results look fabulous. You need to use a heat gun to emboss, so make sure you have an adult's supervision.

What You Need

Stamps
Ink pad
Whatever you want to stamp on
Embossing powder and heat gun*
Scrap paper

*Available in the stamping section of craft stores

What You Do

1 Ink the stamp and stamp it onto your project.

2 While the ink is still wet, sprinkle the embossing powder over it.

3 Tap the excess embossing powder off the project. You can put it back in its container and reuse it later. If you tap the powder onto a piece of scrap paper, you can fold the paper in half and use it as a funnel to pour the extra powder back into the container.

4 Preheat the heat gun for about 10 seconds. Have an adult hold it 4 inches above the project to melt the embossing powder. You'll see the powder melt, rise up, and get shiny. This shouldn't take longer than 15 seconds or so.

5 Once the powder is melted and smooth, turn off the heat gun. Let the stamp cool completely before touching it.

Big Birthday Platter

You don't have to have your own ceramics kiln for this project. Simply check around town for the nearest ceramics studio.

What You Need

Foam birthday stamps
Ceramic paints*
Platter*
Pencil
Small paintbrushes in various sizes

*The paint-your-own ceramics studio will provide these items.

What You Do

1 Ceramics studios that provide unglazed ceramics for you to decorate can be found easily in most areas. Look in the telephone directory under "greenware" or "ceramics" to locate one. Though ceramic studios often have their own stamps you can use, bring your own in case they don't have exactly what you want.

2 It's a good idea to plan your design as much as possible before going to the studio. When you've chosen the piece you want to stamp, use a pencil to mark where you'll place the stamps. The pencil marks will disappear in the kiln.

3 Apply the paint to the candle stamp with a paintbrush. Carefully stamp it on the platter. Brush more paint on the candle stamp, and stamp it as many times as you like.

4 After the paint has dried (it shouldn't take too long), accent the candles by painting on a different color applied with a small brush.

5 Brush the paint on the party hat stamp, and stamp it around the rim. After the paint dries, accent the hats with different colors. You can also accent the hats with a glaze that stands out like puffy paint.

6 Simply leave the platter with the ceramics studio and pick it up when they've fired it.

Sunflower Lampshade

This lampshade will add a little sunshine
(or at least some artificial light) to your life.

What You Do

1 Paint the dark yellow paint onto the petals and the center of the sunflower stamp. Brush one side of each petal with the bright yellow paint and the other side with the orange paint.

2 The tricky part of this project is how to stamp onto the lampshade. Your best bet is to put one hand on the inside of the lampshade to support it, and then stamp the sunflower onto the shade where your hand is located. Make sure you have plenty of paint on the stamp to get a good image. If you need to, touch up the stamped image with the paintbrush.

What You Need

Sunflower stamp
Dark yellow, bright yellow, and orange fabric paint
Small paintbrush
Fabric lampshade
Hot glue gun and glue sticks
Approximately 50 small silk sunflowers
Craft glue
Sunflower seeds

3 Stamp the flower around the entire shade. Let the paint dry.

4 Hot glue the silk sunflowers to the top and the bottom edge of the lampshade. (Be careful not to touch the tip of the glue gun or the hot glue itself.)

5 Use the craft glue to attach sunflower seeds to the center of each stamped sunflower.

Paper Bag Book Cover

What's so great about a brown paper bag? Well, use some found stamps and find out.

What You Need

Bubble wrap, shelf liner with a cool texture, and any mesh-like material to use as stamps
Assorted colors of acrylic paint
Scissors
Brown paper bag
Book to cover
Pencil and ruler
Small piece of paper
Tape
Wax paper
Foam paintbrush
Brayer

What You Do

1 Cut open the paper bag and place it, print side up, on your work surface. Open the book you're going to cover and put it on top of the paper bag.

2 Cut the paper bag 3 inches around the book on all sides.

3 Fold the bag along the top and bottom edges of the book. Crease the edges.

4 Center the book on the bag and fold the edges of the bag over the cover. Set the book aside.

5 Flip the book cover over so the nonprinted side is facing you. If you want to write your name on the cover, tape a small piece of paper onto the front of the book cover where you'd like your name to go.

6 Cut the bubble wrap and the shelf liner to be the length of the book cover. Cut a 2-inch square out of the mesh for the hooked rug.

7 Put the different colors of paint onto the wax paper.

8 Use the foam brush to ink the bubble wrap with whatever color paint you want. Place the stamp on the paper bag and roll over it with the brayer. Repeat with the shelf liner and mesh.

9 After the cover has dried, remove the piece of paper you taped on in step 5. Write your name or the name of your book in there. Cover your book.

THE MONKEY

To make this book cover, get a monkey stamp, a yellow printing pen, and a brown printing pen. Color the face, belly, and hands of the monkey yellow. Color the rest of the monkey brown and stamp it.

Stationery Set

Why buy a stationery set that isn't exactly YOU, when you can make one that perfectly fits your personality?

What You Need

Homemade and store-bought
  stamps
Ink pads in colors of your choice
Blank stationery
Markers
Envelopes and cards
Sticker paper or blank labels
Decorative-edged scissors

What You Do

1 Stamp a single image onto the sheets of stationery. If you want, add further decorations with the markers.

2 Make coordinating envelopes and cards by stamping the same image you used on the sheet of stationery. If you want, stamp the image on the envelope or card several times.

3 Stamp one of the stamps onto the sticker paper to make some fake postage. Draw a square or rectangle around it with the markers.

4 Stamp additional images inside the rectangle you just drew. Use letter and number stamps to make them look like fake postage.

5 Cut around the fake postage with the decorative-edged scissors. Peel off the backing and stick them onto the envelope.

Nature Calendar

Find small items such as flowers, rocks, and leaves to decorate this fun project.

What You Need

Numbers and alphabet stamp sets
Flowers and leaves
Black and colored ink pads
12 sheets of 8½ x 11-inch
   colored card stock
Scissors
Ruler and pencil
12 sheets of 8½ x 11-inch white
   card stock
Glue stick
Scrap paper
Heavy books
Binder clip
Ribbon

What You Do

1 Cut each colored card stock page into 35 rectangles approximately 1 x 1½ inches for each month. Use the ruler and pencil to draw grid lines to make the cutting easier.

2 Assign a color for each month, and stamp the dates in the squares. Make sure you create the correct number of days for each month.

3 Draw a straight line about 3 inches from the top of each sheet of white card stock. Stamp the names of the month on each sheet. Let them dry, and erase the pencil marks.

4 Beginning with January, put the days you created in step 1 into columns so that they're in order starting with Sunday and ending with Saturday. Make sure you put the first day on the right day of the week. (Refer to the correct year's calendar.) Use blank squares on days that don't have numbers.

5 Arrange the days until you're happy with where they are, and glue them in place.

6 Cover the calendar page you just completed with a piece of scrap paper and set a heavy book on top of it. Let it dry for at least an hour.

7 When the calendar page has dried, stamp the letter for each day of the week above the column of dates.

8 Decorate the rest of the calendar page by stamping flowers and leaves on it.

9 Repeat steps 4 through 8 for each month of the year.

10 Put all of the calendar pages in order and attach the binder clip to the top. Thread the ribbon through the back binder clip handle and tie a bow to make a hanger for your calendar. Hang it on the wall.

STAMPING WITH FLOWERS AND LEAVES

If the flowers and leaves you're working with aren't too big, you can use a regular stamp pad. Lightly press the flower or leaf facedown into the stamp pad. Then press the middle and edges of it onto a piece of paper. Practice on scrap paper until you like how your stamps are turning out.

Bug Frames

If you're bugging out, stamp a couple of these cool insects and frame yourself.

What You Need

Grasshopper and ant rubber stamps

Pigment ink pad that can be heat-set on glass (same color as frame)

Wooden picture frame

Dish soap and water

Colored paper (that looks nice with the frame)

Scissors

Photograph that's smaller than the frame

Paper towels

Use of an oven

What You Do

1 Take the glass and backing material out of the frame. Wash the glass with soap and water. Dry.

2 Cut a piece of the colored paper so it fits snugly in the frame. Place the backing, paper, photograph, and glass in the frame. Make sure the photograph is exactly where you want it.

3 Stamp the bugs onto the glass around the photograph. If you don't like the placement of a stamp, wipe it off with a damp paper towel, dry the glass, and try again.

4 Take the glass out of the frame and follow the manufacturer's instructions for setting the ink in the oven. If you want to reverse the stamped images in one frame, simply turn the glass over so the image is facing the back of the frame.

Garden Party

You can make all of the accessories for this party or just a few.
Hey, it's your party.

What You Need

Bug stamps
Alphabet stamp set
White and black stamp pads
Pencil with unused eraser
Scissors
$\frac{1}{16}$-inch hole punch
Glue
Stapler

INVITATIONS

What Else You Need

Green card stock
Plain white greeting cards with
   envelopes

What You Do

1 Cut pieces of the green card stock so each piece is ½ inch smaller all around than the plain white greeting cards.

2 Using the white stamp pad, stamp a bug on each of the pieces of green paper. Use the pencil eraser to color in the stamp. It should be a little bigger than the stamp itself. Let it dry.

3 With the black stamp pad, stamp the same bug on top of the colored-in stamp. Use the alphabet stamps to stamp your message on the bottom of the invitations.

4 Use the $\frac{1}{16}$-inch hole punch to punch a curved flying trail behind the bug (see project photo).

5 Glue the green paper on top of the white cards.

Garden Party

CENTERPIECE

What You Need

Yellow, pink, and
  green card stock
Straws
Vase
River rocks or sand

What You Do

1 Cut twelve 2 x 4-inch rectangles from the colored card stock.

2 Fold the pieces of paper in half, unfold them, and lay them flat on the table.

3 Using the same technique you used for stamping the invitations, stamp a bug on each piece of paper. Create the flying trails with the hole punch.

4 Fold the paper over the tops of the straws, and staple them.

5 Fill the vase with small rocks or sand and put the straws in it to make the centerpiece.

STRAWS

What Else You Need

Yellow and pink card stock
Green straws

What You Do

1 Cut a ½ x 4½-inch piece of yellow or pink paper for each straw.

2 Fold each piece of paper in half to crease it. Unfold it and lay it flat on your worktable.

3 Using the same technique you used for stamping the invitations, stamp a bug on the right-hand side of each piece of paper.

4 Wrap the paper around the straw and staple it together right next to the straw.

5 Use the ¹⁄₁₆-inch hole punch to punch a flying trail behind the bug.

NAPKINS

What Else You Need

Pink paper napkins

What You Do

1 Stamp a bug in white in the top right corner of each napkin.

2 Use the 1/16-inch hole punch to create the flying trail behind the insect.

PLATES

What Else You Need

1/8-inch hole punch
Green paper plates
Hemp string
Yellow card stock

What You Do

1 With the 1/8-inch hole punch, punch an even number of holes around the edge of each plate.

2 Cut a 4-foot length of hemp for each plate.

3 Cut a 2-inch-square piece of yellow card stock to make a name tag for each plate. Using the same technique you used for stamping the invitations, stamp a bug on each piece of paper.

4 Using the alphabet stamps, stamp the name of each person attending the party onto the name tag.

5 Use the 1/16-inch hole punch to punch a flying trail behind the bug. Punch a hole in the top left corner with the 1/8-inch hole punch.

6 Thread the hemp string through the holes in the plate. Put a name tag square on the string. Tie the ends together under the rim of the plate and trim the leftover string.

PARTY HATS

What Else You Need

Pink card stock

What You Do

1 Cut 2-inch-wide strips of paper lengthwise from the card stock. Staple together the narrow ends of two of them for each party guest.

2 Stamp bugs along the strips of paper, about 4 inches apart. Use the same method used for the invitations. Don't forget the flying trails.

3 Form a circle with the strips of paper, and staple the ends together.

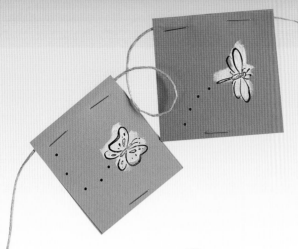

Garden Party

GARLAND

What Else You Need

Pink, yellow, and green card stock
Hemp string

What You Do

1 Cut a length of the hemp string 8 inches longer than the length of the garland you want.

2 Cut the paper into 2½ x 4½-inch pieces. Make three for every foot of garland you're making.

3 Fold pieces of paper in half, unfold them, and lay them flat on the table. Using the same technique you used for stamping the invitations, stamp a bug on each piece of paper. Make flying trails for the bugs.

4 Fold the paper over the garland, alternating the colors and spacing them evenly along the garland. Staple the paper close to the string twice along the top and once on the bottom.

GIFT BAGS

What Else You Need

Yellow card stock
Brown paper lunch bags
Assorted party favors
⅛-inch hole punch
Hemp string

What You Do

1 Cut a piece of 2½ x 3¼-inch yellow paper for each guest.

2 Using the same technique you used for stamping the invitations, stamp a bug on each piece of paper. Make the flying trails.

3 Fill each bag with the party favors. Fold the top of the lunch bag over twice.

4 Place the yellow paper on the front of the bag. With the ⅛-inch hole punch, create two holes through the yellow paper and the front of the paper bag.

5 Cut a 7-inch length of hemp string. Put the paper in place and thread the string through the holes. Tie it off inside the bag and trim the ends.

Awesome Paper Creations

WARNING #1:
These are NOT ordinary paper crafting creations.

Sure, you've probably been cutting, folding, gluing, and doing all sorts of other things with paper ever since your chubby little baby hands could hold onto a pair of safety scissors. But perhaps you weren't aware that paper crafts go way, way beyond cutting out paper hearts and gluing them to shoe boxes. In fact, did you know that with a little bit of glue (yes, the same stuff you liked to let dry on your fingers and then peel off), some newspaper, and a rock, you can make an awesome box that looks like you just dug it out of your garden? Or that, with the same paper you would have used to print out your report on why Godzilla is cooler than King Kong, you can make your very own enveletter? (Or is that a lettervope?) Even that report card you got with a C– in gym class can be turned into art. If you didn't know these things, it's a good thing you're reading this chapter.

WARNING #2:
The paper crafts in this chapter will challenge you, inspire you, and turn you into the creative person you always knew you could be.

Get ready for family and friends to start looking at you differently. Once you start showing off the cool things you can make from paper, family and friends will be saying things like, "You made THAT out of PAPER!? Getouttahere!" People you barely even know will be begging for one of your handcrafted gifts for their birthday. And they (and you) will never again look at paper in the same way. Fantastic!

This chapter shows you how to make several different projects. You'll find instructions for decorating, cutting, and folding paper. After you master the techniques in this chapter, use them to turn your own crafty ideas into reality.

WARNING #3:
You're about to have some serious fun.

If you still think working with paper means gluing strips of paper into loops and making a long chain (yawn), take a moment to flip through this chapter. The projects have been carefully selected so not a single one will be a cause for snoozing.

WARNING #4:
Turn the page NOW! We're done here.

Getting Started

Before you start working on projects, read through this section. It will tell you everything you need to know about the materials and tools you'll be using. You may have to go to a craft or art supply store to find some of these items, but we'll let you know. This section also gives you some helpful hints. Refer back to this section when you need a little help.

THE PAPER

Paper isn't just the white stuff you print your homework out on. There are tons of different kinds of paper in all sorts of different colors, designs, sizes, shapes, and textures. Explore your local art supply, craft, or even office supply stores for fun paper to use for your projects. Here is the lowdown on the types of paper used in many of the projects in this chapter.

Card Stock or Cover-Weight Paper

This paper is bulkier than printer paper. It feels a little like the lightweight cardboard that gift boxes are made of. It holds folds well, so it's great for making things like boxes, and, of course, it's perfect for making cards.

Printer or Photocopy Paper

This *is* the stuff you print your homework out on, though you can find it in a rainbow of colors. It's also known as text-weight paper.

Construction Paper

If you don't know what this is, where were you in kindergarten? Construction paper is great for mosaic projects, weaving, and collage. Because it's cheap, you can use construction paper to do a trial run of your project before using the more expensive paper.

Decorative Paper

This is any type of paper that has a design on it. It can be tissue paper, wrapping paper, wallpaper, or any other cool paper you find. Use it for weaving, folding, cutting, and collage projects.

Vellum

This is a thick, slightly translucent paper you can sort of see through. It holds folds and creases well and lets light show through, so it's perfect for making window hangings, covering candleholders, and decorating other lights. You can also make really fancy party invitations with it.

Origami Paper

This paper is perfectly square and made specifically for traditional paper folding—but you can use it for anything. You can also buy shiny metallic foil and patterned origami paper. Sometimes it's printed on both sides for twice the fun!

From top to bottom: card stock, printer paper, construction paper, and tissue paper

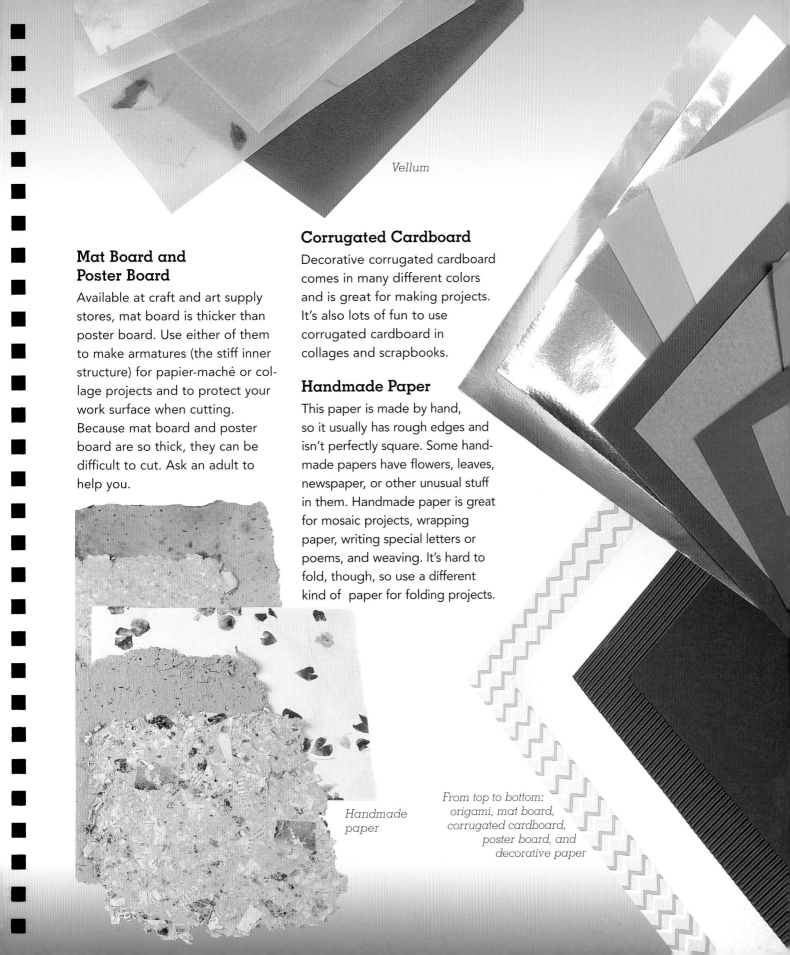

Vellum

Mat Board and Poster Board

Available at craft and art supply stores, mat board is thicker than poster board. Use either of them to make armatures (the stiff inner structure) for papier-maché or collage projects and to protect your work surface when cutting. Because mat board and poster board are so thick, they can be difficult to cut. Ask an adult to help you.

Corrugated Cardboard

Decorative corrugated cardboard comes in many different colors and is great for making projects. It's also lots of fun to use corrugated cardboard in collages and scrapbooks.

Handmade Paper

This paper is made by hand, so it usually has rough edges and isn't perfectly square. Some handmade papers have flowers, leaves, newspaper, or other unusual stuff in them. Handmade paper is great for mosaic projects, wrapping paper, writing special letters or poems, and weaving. It's hard to fold, though, so use a different kind of paper for folding projects.

Handmade paper

From top to bottom: origami, mat board, corrugated cardboard, poster board, and decorative paper

OTHER MATERIALS AND TOOLS

Here are some of the basic tools you'll need for working with paper. Many of these tools can be found around the house, and others can be purchased at craft stores or art supply stores. You can also order most of the tools and supplies mentioned here over the Internet.

Metal-Edged Ruler

You can use a metal-edged ruler to measure and tear paper. This tool is also very helpful if you're trying to cut a straight line with a craft knife (see page 76).

Pencil

This is the essential tool for all your marking and measuring needs. Make sure yours has a good eraser that will actually clean up the lines you make (instead of just smearing them around). Keep your pencil sharp so you can make light lines that are easy to erase.

Brushes

Soft-bristled brushes will help you spread glue where you need it to go. Remember to wash your brushes out with hot, soapy water as soon as you've finished using them.

Glue

White craft glue dries clear and quickly and is perfect for working with paper. You can use it to hold paper, fabric, cardboard, and small pieces of plastic, metal, and glass together. A glue stick is white craft glue in a tube. It's great for gluing pieces of paper together because the glue is easy to spread evenly over the entire surface. Rubber cement is perfect for sticking paper or fabric to paper and cardboard. Decoupage medium is useful for gluing layers of paper together, especially if you're working on a collage. You can make your own decoupage medium by mixing $\frac{2}{3}$ cup of white craft glue with $\frac{1}{3}$ cup of water.

Tape

Cellophane tape is the kind of tape you usually think of when you think "tape." It's clear and can be sticky on one side or both. There are lots of other types of tape. Artist's tape is opaque (not see-through) and is great for holding pieces of paper in place temporarily. It's easy to peel off without messing up the paper.

Scissors

Ah…scissors—possibly the greatest tool ever invented. Many people who work with paper have a pair of scissors they use only for cutting paper. This keeps the blades sharp so that every cut looks great. Keep your favorite pair of scissors close at hand when you're working with paper and well hidden when you're not. Decorative-edged scissors create funky edges when you cut with them and come in all different styles.

Create some funky designs with decorative-edged scissors.

Craft Knife

A craft knife is like a metal pencil with a blade attached to one end. Use a craft knife for cutting out shapes in the middle of a piece of paper and for cutting in tight spaces. They are very sharp, so talk to a parent about whether or not you should be doing the cutting on a project that needs this tool. Never leave craft knives out where pets or younger kids might find them. See page 76 for more information.

Always place a rubber cutting mat or a thick piece of cardboard underneath the paper you plan on cutting with a craft knife.

Rubber Cutting Mat or Piece of Heavy Cardboard

When you use a craft knife, you'll need to put something beneath the paper you're cutting. This will make your cuts neater, keep your blades sharper, AND keep you from cutting up your work surface. (Craft knives are sharp enough to slice into wood, plastic, and countertops.) Rubber cutting mats are ideal because they "heal" themselves—your craft knife won't leave permanent slices in a rubber cutting mat. You can also use a piece of heavy cardboard.

Plates, Bowls, Cups, and Other Round Objects

These are great for helping you draw curved lines and circles to cut out.

Bone Folder

This is a tool made for scoring and folding paper (see page 74). If you don't want to buy one, you can use a butter knife, a ballpoint pen with the ink cartridge removed, or a pair of scissors that is rounded off at the tips. (Yes, just like the ones you used in kindergarten.)

Hole Punches

Hole punches are a great way to decorate paper. They come in all sorts of different styles: from a simple circle to stars, hearts, and flowers. You can use them to punch shapes out of your project, or use the punched-out shapes themselves to decorate your project.

Although you don't need one for the projects in this book, some projects will be easier to do if you have a paper cutter. If you have one, great; however, make sure you have an adult help you use it.

WORKING WITH PAPER

Sure, it may *seem* simple to fold, cut, and glue paper, and you know what? It really is! So why read about it? Well, because the more care you take with your folds and cuts, the happier you'll be with your projects. Here are some tips on how to be an expert paper manipulator.

Orienting the Paper

1 Take a piece of 8½ by 11-inch paper and put it in front of you. The 11-inch side is the length. (Remember, long = length.) The 8½-inch side is the width.

2 To fold the paper *length-wise*, fold the paper in half so that you have a 4¼ x 11-inch sheet of paper (photos 1 and 2).

3 To fold the paper *widthwise*, fold it in half so you have an 8½ x 5½-inch sheet (photos 3 and 4).

Special Tip

When you're folding a piece of paper lengthwise, the length of the paper will stay the same. When you're folding a piece of paper widthwise, the width of the paper will stay the same.

Measuring Paper

1 To measure paper, use a straightedge ruler and a sharp pencil. Line up the bottom of the ruler with the bottom edge

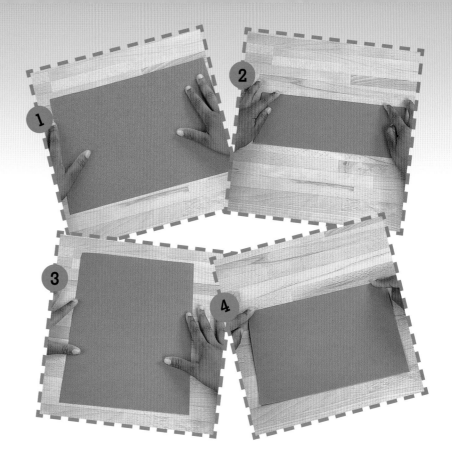

of the paper, and make a light horizontal mark at the correct measurement.

2 Move the ruler to the middle of the paper and measure the distance again (photo 5).

3 After marking that distance, move the ruler to the opposite side of the paper. Measure and mark the paper again.

4 Now that you've made at least three marks (if you're cutting a really big distance, make more marks), line up the edge of the ruler with the marks that you've made.

5 Draw a light line along the side of the ruler (photo 6). That's your cutting line.

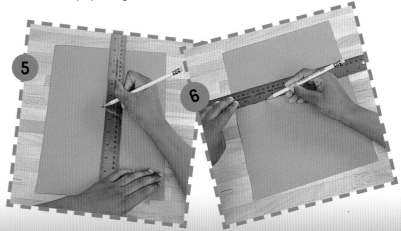

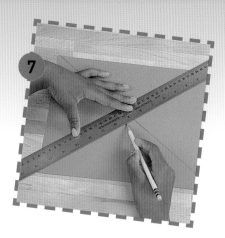

Finding the Center

1 To find the center of a square or rectangular piece of paper, line up the edge of the ruler with the two opposite corners. Make a light pencil mark along the ruler.

2 Move the ruler so that it lines up with the other two corners. Mark the center where the ruler crosses the first line you made (photo 7).

Folding, Scoring, and Creasing Paper

Sometimes all you need to do to fold a piece of paper is to fold it. Other times, however, a more complicated fold will take a little more work. Here's how it's done.

1 Whenever you want to make absolutely sure your fold will be perfect, use your metal ruler as a guide, and mark a line where you want the paper to fold with a few light pencil dots (photo 8).

2 Next, you'll want to *score* the line, which means you'll actually break the top fibers in the paper, making it easier to fold. You can score the line by running the pointed end of a bone folder, butter knife, or empty ballpoint pen along the line, using the metal ruler as a guide once again (photo 9).

3 Fold the paper along this line (photo 10). If the paper doesn't fold easily on the first try, score the line again.

4 To *crease* the fold means to press it down so it'll hold. To do this, hold the paper down with one hand. With the other hand, work from the middle of the foldout (photo 11). You can use the bone folder or butter knife for this. If you don't have either, use your fingernail.

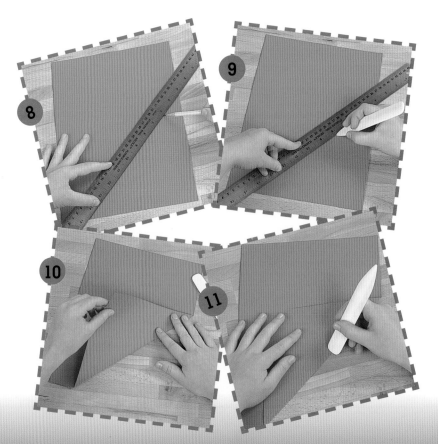

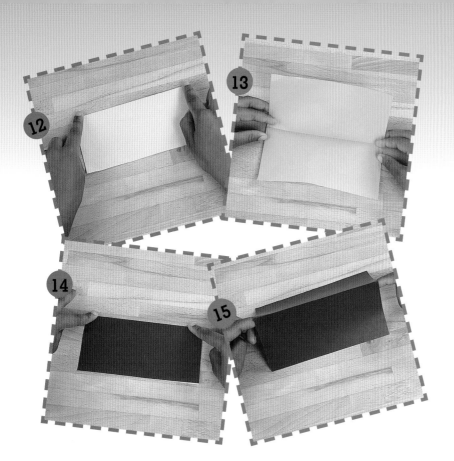

2 Start at one end and fold a section of the paper on top of itself. Flip the paper over and fold another section the same size. (photo 16)

3 Flip the paper over and fold it again. Make sure that all of your crease lines match up (photo 17).

4 Continue to fold and flip the paper until you've folded the entire length. Does it look anything like an accordion (photo 18)?

Valley Folds

Valley and mountain folds are two of the most essential folds for working with paper.

1 To make a valley fold, put your piece of paper patterned-side up in front of you.

2 Fold one half of the paper over the other half and crease the fold (photo 12).

3 Open it up. The piece of paper looks like a valley (photo 13).

Mountain Folds

1 To make a mountain fold, put your piece of paper patterned-side down in front of you.

2 Fold one half of the paper over the other half and crease the fold (photo 14).

3 Open it up and flip the paper over so it is patterned-side up. The piece of paper looks like a mountain (photo 15).

Accordion Folds

1 To make an accordion fold, put your piece of paper in front of you. (It doesn't really matter which side is up.)

Cutting with Scissors

1 When cutting paper, measure and mark the lines you want to cut.

2 Cut along the entire length of the blade; then open the scissors and move the paper toward them. This strategy will keep your cuts straight (or curved if that's what you're doing) and clean.

3 When you're cutting corners, hold the scissors still and rotate the paper to make perfectly cut corners.

Cutting with a Craft Knife

If you want to use a craft knife, make sure you get an adult to help you out.

To cut a straight line with a craft knife, follow these steps:

1 Place a rubber cutting mat or piece of cardboard on your work surface. Place the paper on top of the cutting surface, and use the metal-edged ruler as a guide.

19

2 Hold the craft knife firmly in one hand and press the tip of the knife into the paper.

3 Slowly drag the knife toward you to make the cut, pulling it along the length of the metal-edged ruler (photo 19).

To cut a curved line or a circle with a craft knife, follow these steps:

1 With a sharp pencil, lightly draw the shape you want to cut out.

2 Put your project on a rubber cutting mat or piece of cardboard.

3 Hold the craft knife in your hand like it's a pencil and trace over the line you just drew.

Special Tips

• If you're cutting on top of a piece of scrap cardboard, make sure that you move the paper after each cut you make. If the tip of the craft knife catches in any of the little slices in the cardboard from previous cuts, your paper will tear.

• When using a craft knife, always make sure the hand holding the paper steady is placed above the direction of the cut.

Tearing Paper

1 If you just need to tear pieces of paper that can be any size, just go ahead and start ripping.

2 If you need your pieces of torn paper to be a specific size, place the ruler on top of the paper where you want to tear it.

3 Press it down firmly with one hand and tear the paper with the other hand, starting at the top with a smooth, continuous motion.

Gluing

Here are some helpful hints on how to get the glue on your project (and not on your fingers, in your hair, or all over your workspace and supplies).

1 Cover your work surface in newspaper to keep the glue from getting on things it shouldn't.

2 Use a paintbrush, craft stick, or scrap paper to spread the glue over the base that you'll be sticking the piece of paper onto, or onto the back side of the piece of paper.

3 Position the piece of paper where it goes on the project. Put it down and press the middle of it into place with your fingertips. Press the paper down in the middle and drag your fingers out to one edge. Repeat until you've smoothed over the entire piece of paper. This will remove wrinkles and air bubbles. Wash your glue brush with hot, soapy water.

A Final Note: Using Templates

Several of the projects in this chapter tell you to use templates. If you think your drawing abilities are far superior to ours, go ahead and ignore the templates. If you need a little help, you can do any of the following:

- Tape a piece of tracing paper over the template in the book. Trace all the lines marked on the template. Untape the template and cut it out.

- Lay a piece of tracing paper on the back of the paper you're using for your project. Make sure the chalky side of the tracing paper is facing down. Lay a copy of the template on top of the tracing paper, and trace the shape with a sharp pencil. The image will appear on the project paper.

- Take this book to a copy center. Photocopy and enlarge the template you want to use until it's the right size. Cut off the excess paper.

- Scan the template with a computer scanner, enlarge it if you need to, and print.

Once you have your template all cut out, tape it to the paper or cardboard for your project with artist's tape to hold it in place. You can either use a sharp pencil to trace around the template and then cut it out, or just cut around the template.

Decorating Paper

Sure, you could just dig out your box of broken, half-melted, stubby crayons and start coloring—but why not branch out and try your hand with dyes, special cutting tools, and paints?

In this section, you'll learn fantastic techniques for decorating on and with paper. Fold and dye. tissue paper with food coloring; splatter and sponge paint onto paper; collage layers of paper together; and use pictures, maps, and memorabilia to decorate a box. Use any of the techniques you learn here to make awesome variations on the rest of the projects in the chapter.

orizomegami clipboard

Orizomegami is the ancient Japanese art of folding and dyeing paper. After you learn the technique by making this clipboard, experiment with different ways of folding the paper before dyeing it.

What You Need

Mat board
Ruler
Scissors
Colored tissue paper
Bulldog clip
Food coloring
Cups for food coloring
Paintbrush
Paper towels
   and newspaper
Glue stick
Notepad

What You Do

1 Measure and cut a piece of the mat board to 10 x 14 inches.

2 Cut four pieces of the tissue paper into 6⅕ x 8-inch rectangles. You may want to cut extra rectangles to experiment with.

3 Fold a tissue rectangle diagonally. It doesn't need to be perfect (photo 1). Make an accordion fold across the triangle, making sure that the edge of each

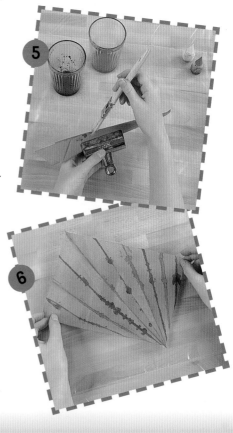

into the food coloring, and blot the excess food coloring onto a paper towel. Brush color along one edge of the folded tissue paper (photo 5).

6 Move the clip to the edge of the tissue paper you just dyed and repeat the painting process. Wash your paintbrush well before switching to a new color.

7 Remove the clip and pull the tissue paper open from the opposite corners (photo 6). Place the paper between two clean pages of newspaper and press out the excess coloring. Let it dry. Repeat steps 3 through 7 with the other pieces of tissue paper.

8 Carefully line up the edges of the pieces of dyed paper on top of the mat board. The tissue paper will overlap the outer edge of the mat board a little bit. Glue the paper to the mat board.

9 Flip the mat board over and glue the overlapping edges of the tissue paper to the back of the mat board.

10 Use the bulldog clip to attach the notepad to the top of the clipboard.

new fold is even with the previous edge (photos 2, 3, and 4).

4 Clip one side of the paper with the bulldog clip so that the folds stay tight.

5 Place food coloring into the cups, using a different cup for each color. Dip the paintbrush

Shake-It-Up Journal

When you get bored with your new journal cover, simply give it a shake or two for a brand new look.

What You Need

Journal or notebook
Ruler and pencil
Blue, yellow, and green card stock
Scissors
White vellum
Orange sewing thread
Sewing needle
Paper clips or clamps
Decorative paper punch
Black fine-tip marker
Glue stick
Waxed paper
Heavy book

What You Do

1 Measure the size of the journal cover. Write down the measurement so you don't forget it.

2 Cut a piece of the blue card stock 1 inch smaller all around than the size of the journal. (For instance, if the cover of your journal is 8 x 10 inches, you'll cut your blue card stock to be 6 x 8 inches.)

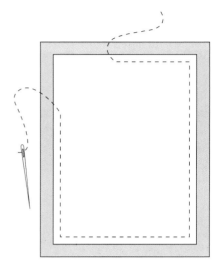

figure 1

3 Cut a piece of the vellum ½ inch smaller than the size of the card stock you just cut. (If your blue card stock is 6 x 8 inches, you'll cut your vellum to be 5 x 7 inches.)

4 Cut a long piece of sewing thread and thread it through the needle. Double your thread, and tie a double knot in the end.

5 Center the vellum on top of the card stock. Use the paper clips or clamps to hold the vellum in place while you sew the papers together. You'll have to move the clips around as you sew.

6 To sew the pages, start at one of the corners. Stick the needle through the back side of the blue card stock and the vellum. The double knot you tied in step 4 should keep the thread in place. Sew through both layers of paper, leaving one corner unstitched (figure 1).

7 With the paper punch, punch out six or seven (or more!) shapes from the yellow card stock.

8 With the marker, write your name in one of the corners of the green card stock. Cut it out. If your journal is actually a notebook for a class, you can create a green class label as well.

9 Slip the piece of card stock with your name on it and the paper punches into the pocket you've made out of the vellum and card stock. Finish stitching the corner closed.

10 Tie the end of the thread in a knot behind the blue card stock.

11 Glue the back of the blue card stock to the front of the journal. Make sure it's centered, and cover the journal with a piece of waxed paper. Put a heavy book on top of the journal and let it dry overnight.

Dream Travel Box

What You Need

Images from magazines, books, brochures, or the Internet
Scissors
Map of your trip location
Shoe box or other box with lid
White craft glue
Foam brush
Decoupage medium

What You Do

1. Cut out the images you want on the box from the materials you've gathered.

2. Glue pieces of the map to the box. You can also simply wrap the bottom of the box with the map.

3. Decorate the rest of the box as you want.

4. Cover the box and lid with a thin layer of decoupage medium to seal and protect your collage.

5. Fill your box with mementos or information that can help you get to your dream location someday.

Planning a trip? Create this collaged box to help you gather information on your location. Just back from a most magnificent vacation? Use mementos to decorate a box of memories.

Add Pizzazz to Scrapbooks

With little more than a few stamps and some ink pads, you can turn any scrapbook or photo album into a fun-filled memory book.

Here are some tips for decorating your pages with stamps:

- Stamp captions to the photos on the page with letter stamps.

- Remember when things happened by stamping the dates onto the pages.

- Record your thoughts and feelings by writing about them with letter stamps or carving stamps that reflect your feelings.

- Use stamps to make frames around the pictures.

- Stamp backgrounds to the pages with found objects that have cool textures.

- Stamp on the pages with a piece of sponge to create cool backgrounds. You can use a regular sponge for this or the special sponges sold at craft stores.

- Glue or stamp leaves and flowers on your pages.

- Make peek-through windows by cutting a hole in the page in front of where you will put the photo or stamp. Then position whatever you want to have peeking through the window on the next page and glue it into place.

Sponge-Painted Photo Album

Create this cool album to hold your favorite pictures from a class trip, family vacation, or any other special time in your life.

What You Need

Card stock in colors of choice
Acrylic paint
Newspaper
Small sea sponge*
Waxed paper
Dish soap
Polka-dot lightweight paper
Scissors
Ruler and pencil
Photographs
Off-white vellum
Glue stick
Hole punch
Key chain

*Available at craft stores

What You Do

1 Decide how many pages you want in your photo album, and also decide which color paint you want to match with which card stock. For this project, we used a lighter or darker shade of paint on a similar color paper. For example, light blue paint on dark blue paper, and purple paint on lilac paper.

2 Lay out some newspaper on the work surface. Wet the sponge and squeeze out the water so it's just damp. Put some paint on the waxed paper and dab the sponge into the paint a few times. Practice dabbing on the newspaper until you get the feel for it.

3 Dab the sponge on the card stock (photo 1). Repeat until you've covered the paper with sponge prints. Repeat with all the colors of paper that you want to use. Wash the sponge with dish soap before changing colors.

4 While the paint's drying, make the photo corners. Cut out several pieces of 1¼-inch-long and ¾-inch-high rectangles from the polka-dot paper (figure 1). Fold up two corners of each rectangle (figure 2). Set these aside.

5 Measure your photos. Cut the card stock into pieces that are 1 inch larger on each side. So, if you're using 4 x 6-inch photos, you'll need a piece of card stock that's 6 x 8 inches. Cut the vellum into pieces that are ½ inch larger on each side. So, if you're using 4 x 6-inch photos, your vellum will be 5 x 7 inches.

6 Glue the vellum to the center of each piece of sponged card stock.

7 Center one of the photographs on the vellum. With the pencil, lightly trace a line around each of the corners. Repeat for all the pages. Glue the photo corners along the lines you traced.

8 Stack the album pages, and punch a hole through all of them in the top left-hand corner with the hole punch. Place your photos in the album, loop a key chain through the holes, and fasten it.

figure 1

figure 2

Pretty Paper

Livening up a normal piece of paper is easy! Use any one of the techniques described next to decorate your paper before you turn it into one of the projects in this chapter.

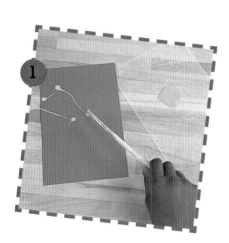

SPLATTERING

What Else You Need

Stiff-bristled paintbrush
Paint
Paper

What You Do

1 Load the paintbrush with the paint.

2 Flick it at the paper (it's all in the wrist!), scrape the bristles with a knife, or tap on the handle of the brush to splatter paint onto the paper (photo 1).

BREEZY WATERCOLOR TECHNIQUE

What Else You Need

Watercolors
Paper
Straw

What You Do

1 Paint some of the watercolor onto the paper (photo 2). The wetter and runnier it is, the better.

2 Blow the watercolor around on the paper with the straw (photo 3).

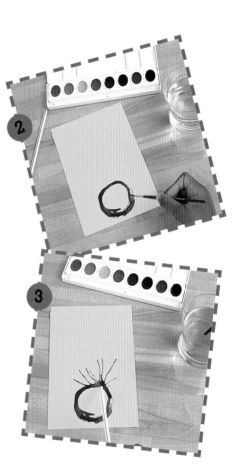

STAMPING

What Else You Need

Rubber stamp
Inkpad
Paper

What You Do

1 Press the stamp into the inkpad. Make sure all of the raised parts of the stamp are covered in ink.

2 Carefully set it on the paper where you'd like it to go. Press evenly over the back of the stamp. Pick it up (photo 4). Tah-dah!

STENCILING

What Else You Need

Stencil
Artist's tape
Paper
Paint and paintbrush

What You Do

1 Tape the stencil in place on the paper (photo 5).

2 Dab the paint into the outlines of the stencil with the paintbrush (photo 6). Don't paint with it—you'll push the paint underneath the stencil.

3 Let the paint dry before removing the tape and stencil (photo 7).

RUBBING

What Else You Need

Paper
Neat texture
Unwrapped crayon

What You Do

1 Put the paper over the neat texture (photo 8).

2 Rub the crayon all over the paper. The texture will be transferred onto the paper (photo 9).

BUBBLING

What Else You Need

½ cup dishwashing soap
1 cup water
Food coloring
Container*
Straw
Paper

*The shape of the container will be transferred onto the page, so find a cool container!

What You Do

1 Mix the dishwashing soap, water, and food coloring together in the container. Add enough food coloring to change the color of the water.

2 Use the straw to blow bubbles in the container (photo 10).

3 Hold the paper over the bubbles, just barely touching the foam (photo 11). As the bubbles burst against the paper, they'll leave a colored imprint on it (photo 12).

4 Pull the paper off the glass and let it dry before making another bubble imprint (photo 13).

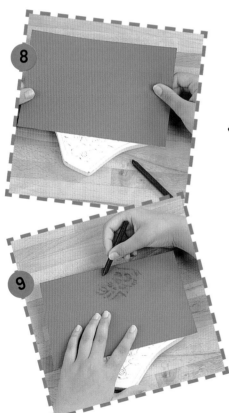

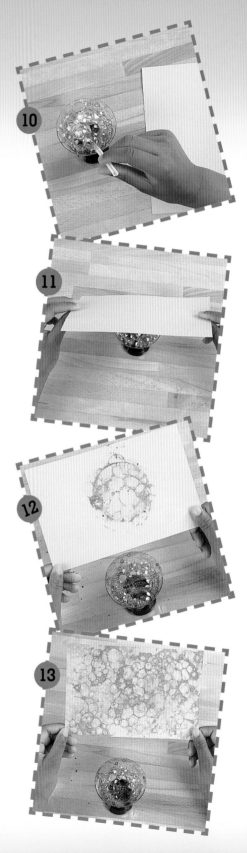

Pet Silhouettes

You can do this project with pictures of just about anything, although, those pets sure look cute.

What You Need

Photograph of your pet's profile
Pencil
Artist's tape
Black paper
Craft knife (see safety tips on pages 71 and 76)
Scissors
Glue
Background paper
Picture frame

What You Do

1 If you don't have a photograph of your pet in profile, see if you can take one. Once the film's processed, you can start.

2 Enlarge the photograph on a photocopy machine to the size of the silhouette you want to create.

3 Outline the profile of your pet with the pencil to define the lines (photo 1). You can outline any details you wish, such as droopy ears.

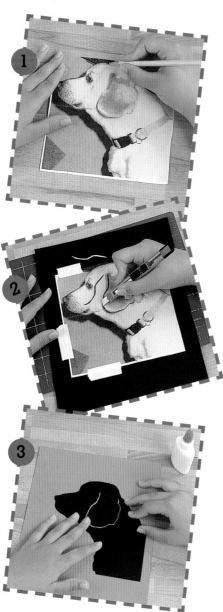

4 Tape the photocopy on top of the black paper. Carefully cut along the outline of any inside details (such as droopy ears) with the craft knife. Then, make a second cutting line just a little bit away from the first cut (photo 2). Lift up the sliver of cut paper with the tip of the craft knife. If the cut doesn't show off the ear or other detail, cut another little sliver. (You can skip this step if you wish).

5 Use the scissors to cut out the outline of your pet. For best results, move the paper, not the scissors, when you turn corners. Take your time.

6 Glue the silhouette to the background paper (photo 3). Use bright colors or a neutral background. Place it in a frame.

Garland

This garland's so easy to make that you'll have plenty of energy left over afterward to party!

What You Need

Colored card stock, 8 x 14 inches
Ruler and pencil
Scissors
Glue stick or tape

What You Do

1 Fold the paper in half lengthwise.

figure 1

2 Use the ruler and pencil to lightly mark a line ½ inch in from each long edge (figure 1).

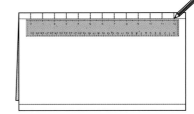

figure 2

3 Starting on the left side of the paper, place the ruler on the ½-inch mark, and create a light mark for every inch (figure 2).

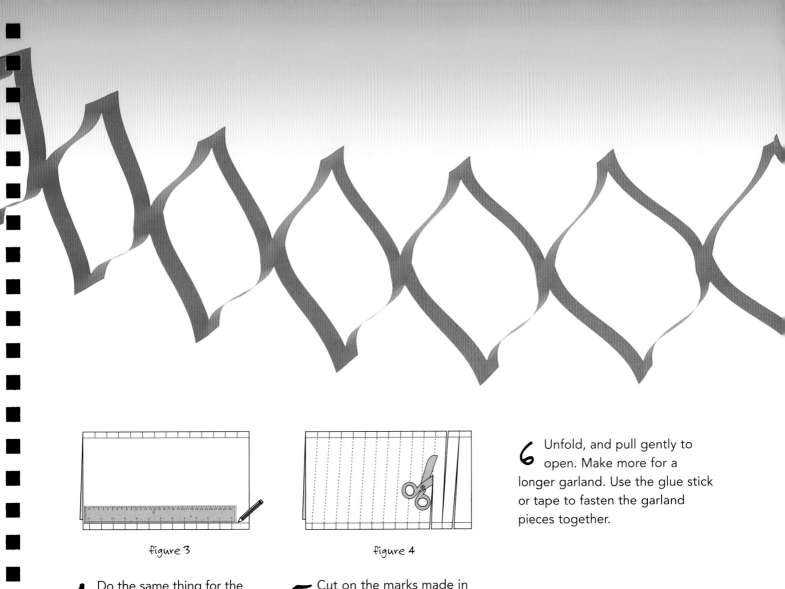

figure 3

figure 4

6 Unfold, and pull gently to open. Make more for a longer garland. Use the glue stick or tape to fasten the garland pieces together.

4 Do the same thing for the right side of the paper, but place the ruler at the bottom of the page and measure and mark every inch from the edge (figure 3).

5 Cut on the marks made in steps 3 and 4, making sure to stop at the ½-inch lines (figure 4).

Holiday Heart Box

Use this box as an envelope or candy holder, or add a handle and create an ornament.

What You Need

1 piece each of red and white vellum, 3 x 8 inches each
Round object such as a cup or bowl
Ruler and pencil
Scissors

What You Do

1 Fold the vellum pieces in half widthwise so that they're 3 x 4 inches.

2 Use the round object and pencil to mark a half circle at the nonfolded end of each piece of paper. Cut out the curve.

3 Starting at the folded edge, cut two slits in each piece

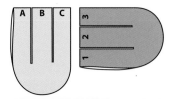

figure 1

of paper 1 inch apart and 3¼ inches long (figure 1). Lightly label the loops as shown in the illustration if you want.

figure 2

4 To weave the first row of the box refer to figure 2. Insert loop 1 into loop C. Then insert loop B into loop 1. Then insert loop 1 into loop A.

figure 3

5 For the second row, refer to figure 3. Insert loop C into loop 2. Insert loop 2 into loop B, and loop A into loop 2.

6 For the third row, insert loop 3 into loop C, loop B into loop 3, and loop 3 into loop A.

7 If you want a handle for your heart box, cut a strip of paper from one of the leftover sheets of vellum, and glue the ends of the handle to the top of the basket on the inside.

Place Mat

Make enough of these wild-looking place mats for your whole family.

What You Need

Ruler and pencil
Colored poster board
Scissors
Scrap cardboard
Craft knife (see safety tips on
  pages 71 and 76)
2 pieces of plain paper
Tempera paints
Paintbrush
Scissors
Glue
Lamination paper or clear self-
  adhesive shelf paper (optional)

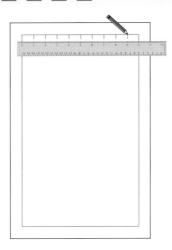
figure 1

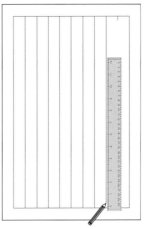
figure 2

What You Do

1 Measure a 12 x 18-inch rectangle on the poster board, and cut it out.

2 Working on the back side of the poster board, measure and draw a 1-inch-wide border around the entire rectangle.

3 Measure and mark lines every inch along the length of the rectangle within the border (figures 1 and 2).

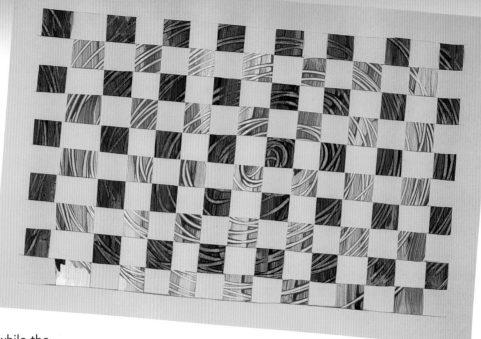

4 Place the poster board, face up, on top of the scrap cardboard. Carefully cut out the lines you drew in step 3 with the craft knife. Don't cut into the border going around the paper.

5 Paint patterns on both pieces of plain paper. Use contrasting colors to make a fun, abstract design and, if you want, while the paint is still wet, use the eraser end of a pencil to create a wavy line in the paint.

6 When the papers are dry, cut them lengthwise into 1-inch-wide strips.

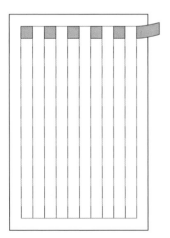

figure 3

7 Select a colored strip to begin weaving with. Weave the strip of paper over the first strip of poster board and under the next (figure 3). Continue alternating over and under until you've finished weaving the strip. Tuck the ends under the border and glue them into place.

8 Select a contrasting colored strip of paper and continue weaving. This time, start by going under the first strip of poster board.

9 Continue this weaving pattern until there is no more room. Slide each strip up so that it fits snugly and neatly next to the previous one.

10 Make sure the ends of all the strips are tucked neatly under the border and glued in place.

11 Either bring the place mat to an office supply store to have it laminated, or laminate it yourself.

12 To laminate it, cut a piece of the lamination or shelf paper slightly larger than the place mat. Peel off the backing and place it sticky-side up onto your work surface. Carefully place the mat on the paper and smooth it down. Cut a second piece and place it on top of the place mat. Cut around the edges until the lamination or shelf paper is the same length around the mat.

Folding Paper

It's physically impossible to fold a piece of paper in half nine times in a row. (Don't believe us? Go ahead and try it.) When you're done trying, check out this section on folding paper. You'll learn a few of the millions of other ways to fold paper.

You'll learn to fold a bracelet, a book so small you can wear it as a necklace, a box, and more. You can fold paper to make decorations for your room, or presents for your friends. (So give up on the "in half nine times in a row" thing. We told you it's impossible!)

Paper-filled ornaments

Make sure to use lightweight papers that have color or patterns on both sides, since you'll be seeing both sides in the ornaments.

What You Need

Fancy papers, 8½ x 11 inches each
Scissors
Clear glass ball ornaments*

*Available at craft supply stores

What You Do

1 Cut one sheet of paper into thirds, so that each strip is 8½ inches long and 3⅔ inches wide.

2 Fold one of the strips accordion-style the long way (so you'll have an accordion-folded strip that's 3⅔ inches wide). Make the folds about ¼ inch apart. Do this for all three of the strips.

3 Hold one folded strip in one hand and cut it into ¼-inch pieces. You should get about 14 strips from each piece of accordion-folded paper.

4 Follow steps 1 through 3 for each sheet of paper.

5 Pull all the folded strips open slightly. Take the tops off the ornaments, fill them with strips of paper, and put the tops back on.

Paper Bouquet

Buy lots of different
colored tissue
paper and make
all of your
favorite flowers.

What You Need

2 pieces of purple tissue paper,
   15 x 20 inches
2 pieces of yellow tissue paper,
   7½ x 20 inches
Heavy floral wire, 18 inches long
   for each flower*
Scissors

*Available at craft stores

What You Do

1 Fold all of the pieces of tissue paper in half lengthwise to mark their centers (photo 1). (This will make it easier to keep them all lined up.)

2 Stack the four pieces of tissue paper together so that the smaller pieces are on top of the larger ones. Make sure their center lines match up. Place the paper pile in front of you widthwise, and accordion fold about 1 inch apart (photo 2).

3 Fold the piece of floral wire in half, slip it around the center of the folded tissue papers, and wrap the ends of the wire together to hold the fold in place (photo 3).

4 Cut along the ends and tops of the folds on the outside edge of the purple tissue paper to make petals (photo 4).

5 Gently pull the top page out to open the flower (photo 5). Shape the petals with your fingers as you open them. Open the rest of the flower in the same way.

Variations

You can create different flowers by altering colors, the sizes of the sheets of tissue paper, and the petal cuts. Here are some examples:

Black-Eyed Susan: Use yellow for the petals and black for the center.

Mexican Sunflower: Use orange and red half-sheets for the petals and gold for the center.

Fantasy Flower: Use silver for the petals and black for the center.

Sunflower: Use brown for the center and make it larger so that just the outside ends of the petals show.

Red-Fringed Poppy: Use red for the petals, but don't cut them, since poppy petals aren't distinct. Make the center out of two 5 x 7½-inch sheets of black. Cut halfway to the center to make the edges look fringed.

Animal Print Box

This little box is the purrfect place to hide your wild things.

What You Need
Ruler and pencil
Scissors
2 pieces of 8½ x 11-inch
  animal print paper or
  lightweight card stock
Glue stick (optional)

What You Do

1 Measure and cut an 8-inch square from the animal print paper.

2 With the ruler and pencil, mark the center of the square on the back side of the paper.

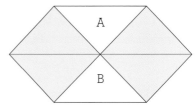

figure 1

3 Fold two corners opposite one another to the center and make nice creases (figure 1). These two corners are now triangles A and B.

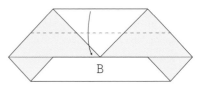

figure 2

4 Fold the two corners you just folded (A and B) into the center again (figure 2). The flat edges of the fold should meet. Crease both of the new folds well.

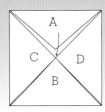

figure 3

5 Open up the last fold you made, then fold the other two corners (triangles C and D) into the center and crease them (figure 3).

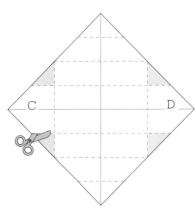

figure 4

6 Unfold the paper so that it's an 8-inch square again. Look carefully at the fold lines. Find the four small triangles formed by the fold lines (figure 4). Carefully cut them out.

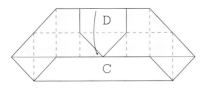

figure 5

7 Fold triangles C and D into the center. Fold them into the center again so that their flat edges meet (figure 5). Crease those folds well and open them up all the way.

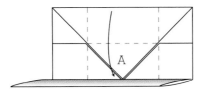

figure 6

8 Fold triangles A and B into the center. Fold them into the center again so that their flat edges meet. Open them up halfway, keeping the points of the triangles in the center (figure 6). These are the first two sides of the box.

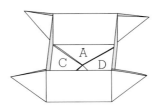

figure 7

9 Fold triangles C and D so that their points meet in the center of the box, and they're forming sides. Your box should now look like figure 7.

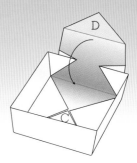

figure 8

10 Reverse the folds of the four triangles to make your box not look like a box. Pull triangle C up and over the reverse-folded triangles (figure 8). Repeat on the other side with triangle D.

11 For the bottom of the box, cut an 7¾-inch square from the second sheet and repeat the instructions from step 2.

3-D Birthday Greetings

Show that you care with style and flair!

What You Need

2 sheets of construction paper or card stock, cut to 5½ x 12 inches
Ruler and pencil
Scissors
Template on page 171
Markers

What You Do

1 Fold each piece of paper in half lengthwise, making sure to match the edges. Open the fold. Fold both ends to the center crease.

2 Stand the two pieces of paper up so that one looks like a **W** and the other an **M** (figure 1).

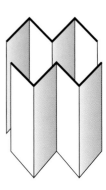

figure 1

figure 2

3 Fold up the **W**. Measure and mark a vertical line up the center of the folded **W**. From the bottom cut 2¾ inches up the line through all four layers (figure 2).

figure 3

4 Fold up the **M**. Measure and mark a vertical line down the center of the folded **M**. From the top cut 2¾ inches down the line through all four layers (figure 3).

5 Lay the **W** down on the table so there are two mountain folds pointing up. (The slits are on the bottom end.)

6 Trace or photocopy the templates on page 171. See page 77 for more information on using templates. Center the candle template on the left mountain fold ¾ inch down from the top of

figure 4

the sheet (figure 4). Trace the candle template. Fold the paper up and cut through both layers with scissors.

figure 5

7 Trace the exclamation template on the right mountain fold ¾ inch down from the top of the sheet (figure 5). Fold and cut through both layers.

8 Take **M** and lay it down on the table so there is only one "mountain" fold. Trace the cake template on the "mountain" fold ¾ inch from the top. Cut through both layers with scissors.

9 Stand up the **M** card, and gently fit the **W** card into the **M** by lining up the slits.

10 Notice the spaces where you can color or decorate behind the cutouts. Mark these areas so you can be sure which parts to color when you take apart the card.

11 Take apart the card. Color and decorate it with the markers. Then, gently put the card back together and fold it shut.

The Amazing Enveletter

Or is it a lettervope? Either way, this two-in-one letter AND envelope is fun to send and read.

What You Need

8½ x 11-inch piece of paper
Pencil and ruler
Markers, crayons, rubber stamps, or other decorations

What You Do

1 Place the sheet of paper widthwise in front of you. Write a letter to a friend, parents, or a pen pal. Decorate the other side.

figure 1

2 With the pencil and ruler, lightly draw a line 2½ inches from the top left edge (figure 1).

figure 2

3 Fold the top right corner to meet the line you drew (figure 2).

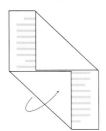

figure 3

4 Fold the lower left corner to meet the lower edge of the top fold (figure 3).

figure 4

5 Fold the bottom right corner so that it's flush with the left edge (figure 4).

figure 5

6 Fold the top down so that there's a little triangle below the fold, making sure to line up the right edges together (figure 5).

figure 6

7 Fold the tip over to the front (figure 6). Address the envelope, add a stamp, and mail.

Book Necklace

This little book is perfect for recording your observations. Make one like ours in which to draw the world around you, or create your own. Wear it around your neck and you'll always have something to write on.

What You Need

8½ x 11-inch piece of white paper
Ruler and pencil
Scissors
Manila file folder
Stapler
Thin nail
Ribbon
Colored pencils, crayons, or markers
Glue stick

What You Do

1 Measure and cut a 2¼ x 10½-inch strip from the piece of paper.

2 Measure in 1½ inches from one end of the long paper strip you just cut. Fold the strip at this point. Continue accordion-folding the strip. Fold the paper neatly, and crease each fold well. Set this piece aside.

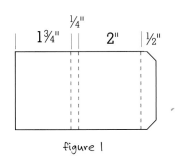

figure 1

3 Measure and cut a 2 x 4½-inch rectangle from the manila file folder.

4 Transfer the measurements shown in figure 1 onto the inside of the manila rectangle. Fold the rectangle and cut the corners as the illustration shows.

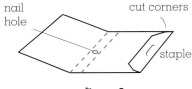

nail hole

cut corners

staple

figure 2

5 Staple once just above the short fold line (figure 2). Glue the last page of the accordion-folded booklet to the back of the folded cover. The longer front flap will tuck into the shorter one when the book is closed (like a matchbook).

6 With the nail, punch a hole in the center of the narrow spine at the top of the book (the space between the back cover and front flap, as shown in figure 2).

7 Cut a length of ribbon long enough to fit over your head. Tie the ends together. Thread the folded end of the ribbon through the hole from the inside out. The knot will catch on the inside of the book.

8 With the pencil, draw small nature images on the left-over manila file folder. Color in the images with the colored pencils, crayons, or markers and cut them out. Glue them to the cover of your book. Draw, doodle, or write to your heart's content.

Interlocking Paper Bracelet

These lovely bracelets are quite easy to make once you get the hang of how the paper pieces slip together.

What You Need

Ruler and pencil

Scissors or paper cutter (and adult supervision)

Recycled paper or thin paper of choice

Bone folder

What You Do

1 Measure and cut 2 x 4½-inch strips of paper. A paper cutter will make this task a lot easier, but make sure you have an adult's help. You'll need about 24 strips. Cut a few extra strips while you're at it.

2 Fold a strip in half lengthwise (photo 1), and crease the fold with the bone folder or your fingernail. Open up the strip, and fold the two long edges into the center crease (photo 2). Fold this strip in half again (photo 3) lengthwise and crease it with the bone folder.

3 Fold and crease the strip in half at the center (photo 4). Open the folded strip, then fold in each of the two ends to the center (photo 5). Fold the strip in half, as shown (photo 6). Fold all of your strips this way.

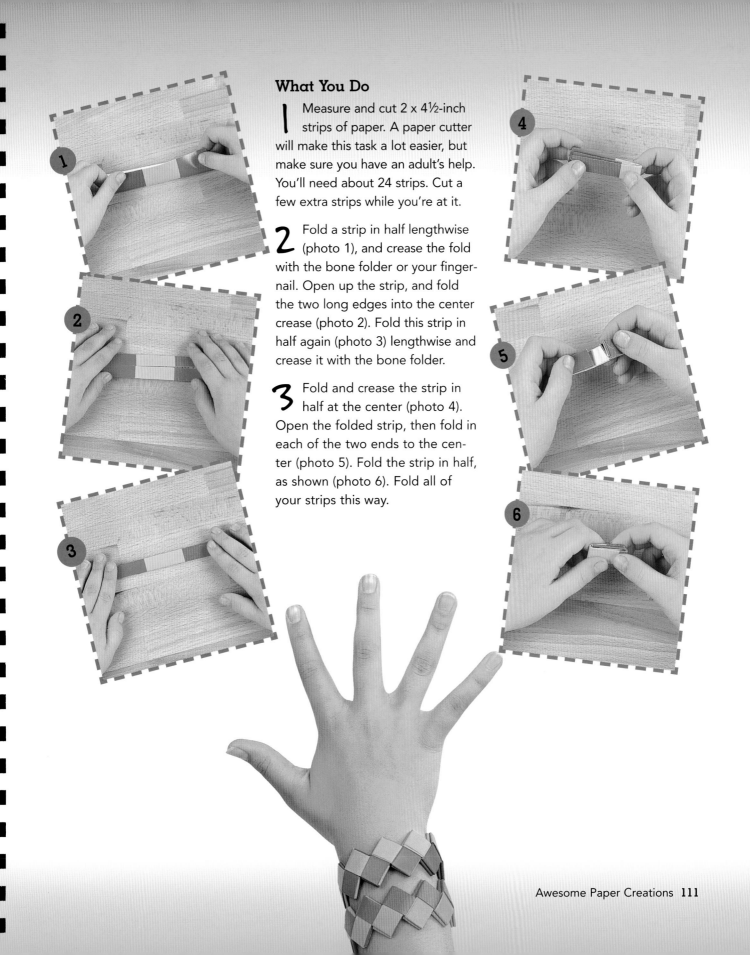

4 Before interlocking the strips into the bracelet, take a moment to look carefully at a folded strip. You will see that one edge is a solid fold (photo 7 top) and the opposite edge is composed of two folded edges (photo 7 bottom).

5 Always look at the folded edges to determine where you're going to interlock a folded strip. The rule is to always insert your folded strips with the solid fold into the edge of the other strip made of one solid fold. Begin by interlocking two strips at right angles to one another. Pull them together snugly (photos 8 and 9).

6 Continue interlocking strips until you have made a chain the length you'll need in order to slip it over your wrist.

7 Pick up one folded slip and unfold the ends. Insert it as if it were just another strip.

8 Pull the chain together snugly. Take each end of the unfolded strip, and slip them into the strip at the end of the bracelet (photo 10). Tuck each end into the middle of the last strip on the bracelet.

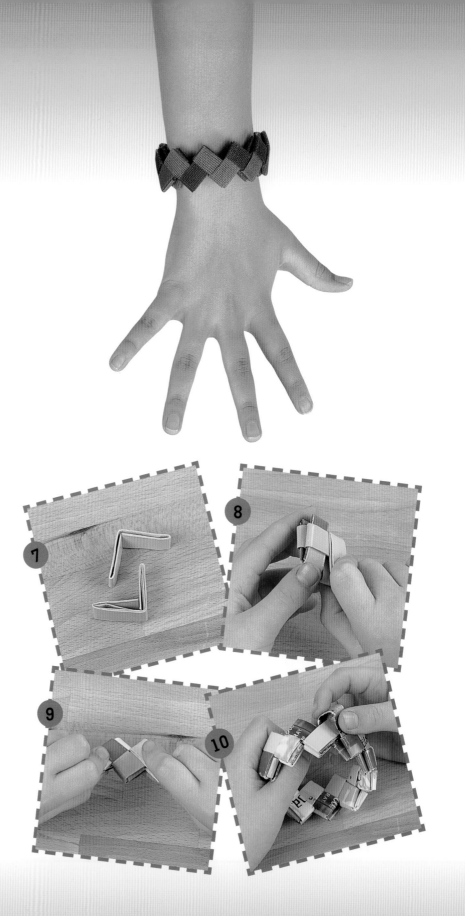

Wrinkly Gift Wrap

Add some flair to your next gift with this fun technique. Experiment with other types of paper, and create little bouquets of paper flowers.

What You Need

2 to 4 sheets of Unryu paper* or other thin paper (bigger than the box you wish to wrap)
½- to ¾-inch-wide ruler or piece of very stiff cardboard
Gift box
Cellophane tape
Glue

*Generally available at art supply stores

What You Do

1 To wrinkle the wrapping paper, wrap the Unryu paper around the ruler or stiff cardboard (photo 1).

2 When all the paper is wrapped around the ruler, push in hard from both ends to produce firm wrinkles (photo 2). Carefully unwrap the paper.

3 Wrap the gift box using the wrinkled paper and tape.

4 To make rosebuds for decorating the box, cut a 3 x 8-inch strip of paper, and wrap it around the ruler widthwise.

5 Unwrap it from the ruler and lay it down lengthwise in front of you.

6 Make two ½-inch folds from the top of the paper.

7 Roll the paper up from one end to make the rosebud (photo 3).

8 When the paper is completely rolled, pinch and twist the thinner section for the stem (photo 4). Attach the rosebuds to the center of the package with glue.

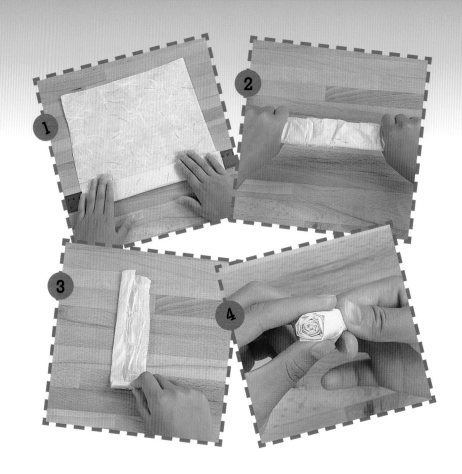

Fabulous Polymer clay objects

POLY WHAT?

Polymer clay is the most fun you'll ever have with a pliable, blend-able polyvinyl chloride suspended in plasticizer.

HUH?

Okay, let me try again.

Polymer clay is a factory-made material that has been around since the 1950s or so (ancient history!). It was invented in Germany for making dolls, and it wasn't until around 20 years later that artists started making colorful beads and jewelry with it. Nowadays, people are doing all kinds of things with it, and more new ideas are being explored every day.

What will you be able to make? What a question! It's more like what *can't* you make with this clay. Put a hole in a piece of clay, and you've got the beginnings of a bead necklace. Sculpt a miniature person, animal, or even a room complete with furniture, curtains, and a vase full of flowers. Cover jars, picture frames, light switch plates, and cabinet knobs. Make a weird bowl, a fat pen, a glow-in-the-dark mobile . . . the list is endless.

WHAT ELSE?

- Polymer clay doesn't dry out like earthen clay, so you can take your time creating with it—in other words, you can keep working until you're happy with your project.

- It comes in tons of colors, and you can create your own.

- You can bake your polymer clay projects in a regular oven, so you don't need a kiln that fires at a high temperature, like the ones ceramic artists use.

- The most important tools you'll need are your hands, and the rest of the tools you'll use are inexpensive and readily available.

So whether you've worked with polymer clay before, or you're hearing about it for the first time right here, this book will show you some pretty awesome things you can make that you probably never ever thought you could do.

One more thing: Please read the next section before starting on any of the projects. It will give you all the information you'll need to do every project in this chapter. Even if you've created with polymer clay before, take some time to check it out.

You've got 13 ideas here in this chapter. Use them as starting points, learn the techniques, create some fun stuff, and never be afraid to let your imagination take over. Ready? Turn the page.

Getting Started

This section will take you through absolutely, positively everything you need to know to get started creating with polymer clay. So, read it before you try working on a project—especially since tools and techniques in the projects' instructions are discussed right here.

Set Up Your Work Area

Artists and craftspeople usually have studios— separate rooms where they work on their projects. Most likely, you won't have that luxury. If you're lucky, however, you might have space in your bedroom or a corner of the basement you can clear out.

After you've found your "studio" space, you need a flat surface, such as an old table, to work on. Don't work on the nice dining room table—the clay can mess up the table's finish, and sharp tools will leave marks. (Someone's sure to get mad if this happens.)

You can work directly on a smooth ceramic tile or a metal cookie sheet so you can move your project directly to the oven when it's ready to be baked. Sometimes it's also handy to put a piece of typing paper down to work on, so it's easy to move the project. Experiment, and find out what works best for you.

POLYMER CLAY

There are two main sections to the instructions for each project in this book: What You Need and What You Do. (Pretty self-explanatory, eh?) The first line or two in the "What You Need" section tells you how much polymer clay you need and the colors used. If you don't like the colors listed, use different ones.

Buy Your Clay

You can find polymer clay at any craft store and many toy stores. There are several different brands of clay available, and each one is slightly different in softness, strength, and color. You can experiment with different brands. You can mix together any of the brands to create new colors or degrees of workability (how soft or hard the clay is). Just make sure you mix them thoroughly. If you don't, the resulting clay may be weak.

Generally speaking, you can buy polymer clay in small, 2-ounce packages and larger, 1-pound bricks.

When shopping for clay:

- Make sure you don't buy clay that's hard.

- Learn which brand works best for you.

- Learn which stores or mail-order suppliers have the freshest clay.

Where to Store Polymer Clay

Besides putting it somewhere that your little brother can't get to it, it's important to keep your unbaked polymer clay away from heat and direct sunlight, both of which may make the clay stiffer and harder to work with. Cover your clay and work-in-progress with wax paper to keep them protected from dust and pet hair.

TOOLS AND OTHER STUFF YOU NEED ...

Most of the stuff you need to work on the projects in this book can be found around your house; however, don't use kitchen utensils unless you have permission. Why not? Because you can't use any tools with food again once you've used them for polymer clay. Without further delay, here's a list of tools and materials you might need.

ROLLING TOOLS

Of the four tools listed below, you only need one. Find the one you like to use best.

Printer's Brayer

This is perhaps the best tool for rolling out clay. You can use either a clear acrylic or black rubber brayer, though the clear acrylic seems to work better. You can find both at craft stores.

Acrylic Rod

This is a hollow or solid clear, plastic rod.

Plastic Rolling Pin

As a last resort, you can use a plastic rolling pin to roll clay. Don't use a wooden one—it leaves marks on the clay, and the wood absorbs the plasticizer.

Pasta Machine

If there's an unused pasta machine around the house, ask if you can have it. It will make rolling sheets of clay a breeze. Pasta machines are also great for conditioning the clay (more about that in a minute), and for combining colors. Though not necessary for the projects in this book, get your hands on one if you can They're fun and easy to use.

CUTTING TOOLS

You'll definitely need the first two of these tools. Please get an adult's help when learning how to use them, and always work carefully and slowly.

Cookie Cutters

These can be used for making shapes out of sheets of clay. Buy your own cutters, or ask a parent whether or not you can take the ones gathering dust in the junk drawer. Cutters are also available at craft stores.

Small Shape Cutters

These are a lot like cookie cutters, but . . . smaller.

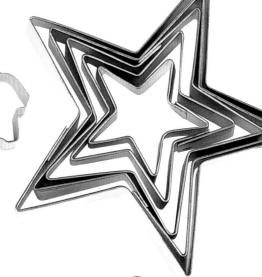

Polymer Clay Cutting Blade

This is a one-sided blade that's perfect for cutting sections of clay or for cutting canes. Look for one in the polymer clay section of a craft store.

Craft Knife

A common craft knife can also be used for cutting clay.

Butter Knife

It doesn't cut as well as either of the other tools; however, for some projects, a butter knife will perform all of your cutting needs just fine.

SCULPTING TOOLS

These tools push, nudge, and coax your clay into place. They fit in places where your pinky finger can't and can make anything from an interesting dotted design to a mouth, nostrils, or eyes.

Toothpick

Your next best sculpting friend is the toothpick. In many cases you can use a toothpick instead of a needle tool.

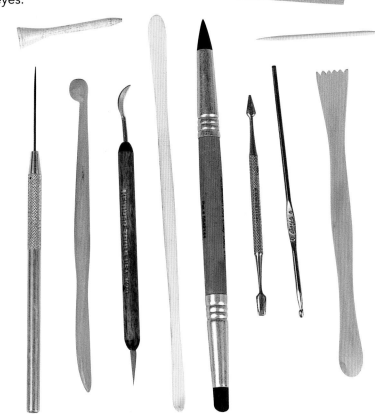

Needle Tool

In the ceramics or pottery section of a good craft store, you'll find a bunch of sculpting tools you can use. One of the handiest is called a needle tool. The long needle on the end of this tool is great for making holes for beads.

Junk Drawer Items

You can also use junk drawer items such as a golf tee, cuticle shaper, crochet hook, bobby pin, paper clip, sewing needle, screw, bamboo skewer, fat knitting needle, and more to sculpt, incise, embellish, and decorate your clay.

TEXTURING TOOLS

Texturing tools are anything you can use to make patterned indentations or impressions in the clay. You can use rubber stamps, sandpaper, scraps of lace, window screen pieces, crumpled wax paper, the back side of a plastic dinosaur, interesting game pieces, and even the clean bottom of a shoe.

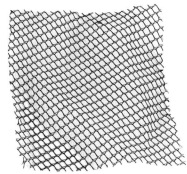

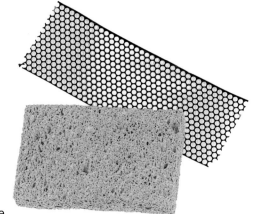

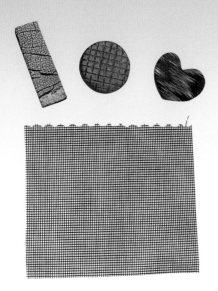

RELEASE AGENTS

When texturing clay, you'll sometimes need a very light application of either powder, cornstarch, or water to keep the texture from sticking to the clay (see page 127).

BAKING TOOLS

Baking your clay in a home oven is simple and one of the main reasons polymer clay is so popular. You need an oven or a toaster oven and the rest of the stuff listed here.

Ceramic Tile, Glass Baking Pan, or Cookie Baking Sheet

You need one of these to place your finished projects in the oven.

Oven Thermometer

An inexpensive oven thermometer is a must, since oven temperatures are not always accurate, and polymer clay is very picky about the temperature.

Polyester Batting or Paper

Most projects call for you to place your project on some polyester batting or a piece of paper for baking. (Don't worry, these materials won't burn at the low temperature at which you'll be baking the clay.) If you don't use them, your project may get a shiny flat spot where it was resting on the baking sheet or tile.

GLUES

Cyanoacrylate glue is an instant-bonding glue you can find at supermarkets and craft stores (for example, Instant Krazy Glue or Super Glue). You'll also need white craft glue (PVA), though make sure it's heat-resistant (Sobo craft and fabric Glue works well). Check the polymer clay section of the craft store, or ask for help finding it.

TOOLBOX

One of the best ways to keep all your tools together and make sure nobody uses them for anything else, is to find or buy a toolbox. This way, you'll know where everything is, and nobody will be tempted to use your cookie cutters to make cookies.

IMPORTANT LIST OF SAFETY TIPS

Okay, we're almost ready to start working that clay, but first, even though polymer clay is certified non-toxic, there are a few safety tips you should be aware of.

- Never microwave your polymer clay!

- Don't snack while you're working with the clay. It's not a good idea to eat any of it, even very small amounts. Besides, you might get cheese puff crumbs in your project!

- Don't rub your eyes, pick your nose, etc. until you've washed the clay from your hands.

- To wash your hands, use regular hand lotion to break down the clay and make it easier to remove from your hands. Rub the lotion off with a terry cloth rag or paper towel, then wash with cold water, soap, and a nail brush to remove all residue.

- The tools you use for polymer clay should be used only for polymer clay. In other words, don't return the pasta machine to the kitchen cabinet once you've run clay through it.

- Ventilate well when baking, and don't breathe the fumes. Be sure to use an oven thermometer to prevent burning. Open a window and turn on a fan if you do end up burning the clay.

- Polymer clay should never be used to make anything to eat or drink out of. No ashtrays or incense burners, either!

WORKING WITH THE CLAY

The instructions for each project tell you exactly what to do in order to design your own polymer clay creation.

There are also lots of step-by-step photographs to show you what is being discussed. But before you start working on the steps, there are a few more things you need to consider.

FIGURING AMOUNTS

Most brands of polymer clay are conveniently marked so you can cut them into equal portions. If you buy blocks that aren't marked, don't worry. Since most amounts listed in the "What You Need" section are approximate, you can usually eyeball how much clay you'll need and be okay.

CONDITIONING THE CLAY

Though some of the polymer clays are kind of soft and workable right out of the package, it's still necessary to squish and squeeze it before you use it. This is called *conditioning*, and not only does it make the clay softer, more malleable, and hence easier to use, but it will also make your finished project stronger. Conditioning ensures that the plasticizer (the stuff that makes the clay soft) is evenly distributed throughout the clay. A project made with unconditioned clay might be weak and could break.

How to Condition Your Clay

• Use your hands, and squeeze about a 1-ounce block until you can roll it into a snake.

• Fold the snake a few times; roll it out again, fold again. Try not to get any air bubbles in your clay when you do this.

• Roll and fold until you can pull the ends of the clay and it stretches instead of breaks.

• If you're also mixing colors, conditioning is the perfect time to do it since you use the same process for both.

Using a Pasta Machine

Conditioning with a pasta machine is a cinch! Most models come with a clamp you can use to secure the machine to your work table.

• Cut up your block of clay into slabs no thicker than ¼ inch. If the clay is too thick, you'll damage the machine.

• Set the machine at its thickest setting (#1 on most models), and roll your clay through.

• Fold the sheet and repeat. Keep doing this until the clay stretches when pulled.

• When you put the folded clay through the pasta machine, be sure the fold isn't on the top edge, or you'll trap air in the fold.

CHOOSING & MIXING COLORS

Although polymer clay comes in a huge variety of colors, if you can't find the color you want, you can mix clays to create nearly any color. You can combine colors randomly, adding a pinch of this and a smidgen of that until you've got a color you like. Or follow these guidelines for creating your own color recipes:

- Combine yellow and blue to get green.

- Combine red and blue to get purple.

- Combine yellow and red to get orange.

- To darken a color, add a small amount of black.

- To lighten a color or make it look more pastel, start with white and add color to it.

- If you vary the proportions of the colors in the mixture, you'll get colors such as bluish green or pale orange.

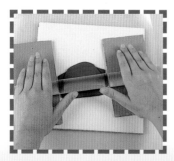

ROLLING OUT YOUR CLAY

In the "What You Need" section, whenever you need a rolling tool it will say "Rolling tool or pasta machine."

Experiment with rollers, if you can, until you have one you like best. Just about every project will tell you to first roll your conditioned clay into a sheet. That means taking a small, thick clump of clay and rolling it out thin, as you would cookie dough. Sometimes I like to put the clay between two pieces of wax paper to keep the clay from sticking to the roller. Then, it's a simple matter of rolling until the clay is the thickness and size you want. Roll back and forth and then side to side; flip it over and roll some more. This will result in a more even sheet. To roll out a ⅛-inch thick sheet of clay, first place two pieces of cardboard on either side of the clay you're about to roll.

Rolling with a Pasta Machine

Many of the sheets you'll roll will be ⅛-inch thick (the thickest setting on the machine). That's about the same thickness as a piece of cardboard.

Always start rolling at the thickest setting, and if you need a thinner sheet, set the machine one or two notches thinner each time. If you go from thickest to thinnest right away, you'll damage the machine. Refer to page 125 for further instructions.

CUTTING THE CLAY

After rolling out your clay, you'll sometimes be asked to cut it. The tools listed on page 121 are all you need to do all the cutting in this chapter. Make sure you're always careful with these tools, and don't leave them around the house for your far less responsible younger siblings to play with.

Using a Craft Knife

A craft knife is helpful for cutting simple designs. Hold the craft knife firmly in one hand, and press the tip of the knife into the clay. Slowly drag the knife to make a cut.

Using a Polymer Clay Cutting Blade

This tool is good for cutting canes (more on that on page 121) and cutting straight lines in the clay. Since it only has one sharp edge, you can hold it by its blunt edge, and you won't hurt your hand. See the photo below for the best way to hold it.

COOL TRICKS

The rest of the project instructions will show you what to do next. If the instructions mention a technique you're not familiar with, simply turn back to this section, and read the instructions for that technique. You'll learn lots of different ways to decorate your clay projects. Some are simple, and some require a little more patience and practice. Here they are, in no particular order.

Texturing

Texturing creates fun surfaces for your polymer clay projects, so they feel and look great. Do you want your clay to look sort of rough? Press sandpaper into the surface. Looking for a geometric pattern? Use a small piece of window screen or lace. Start collecting cool texturing tools in your toolbox.

Keeping the Clay from Sticking to Your Texture

Sometimes the polymer clay will stick to the texturing item or even to your tools. When that happens, you can spread a little cornstarch on the clay with your

fingertip. You can also just dip your fingertip into a bowl of water, and rub it onto the clay. Either way will allow the texture to do its job without sticking.

Marbling

Marbling is something we do with polymer clay almost instinctively. Twist and turn two or more colors together until you like how it looks. Don't overdo it, or the colors will start to blend together, and you might get mud.

Embedding

Embedding simply means sticking objects into the clay. You can push them in all the way or leave them sticking out a bit. There are so many things you can embed into your clay projects, it would be impossible to list them all here. If you don't think your object will stick, make a small indentation in the clay, dab a little bit of heat-resistant PVA glue on the object, and gently place the object into the indentation. If objects fall out after baking, simply place a dot of cyanoacrylate glue on the object and try again. If you think the object might melt when baking, just glue it in place afterwards.

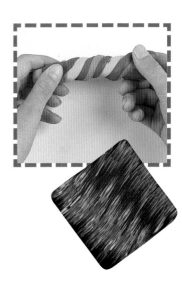

Onlay

When you add small pieces of clay to the surface of another piece of clay and leave them sticking up a little, it's called *onlay* or *appliqué*. You can use cut-out shapes, tiny balls you roll between your fingers, or slices from canes. You can build up layers, too. Press the pieces of onlaid clay enough to make them stick, but not so much that you squish them.

Covering Surfacing

Sometimes you may want to cover a surface or object that polymer clay does-n't want to stick to, such as wood or metal. It's easy to fix that! Apply a thin coat of heat-resistant PVA glue to the wood or metal, allow it to dry, and put your clay on that. Polymer clay will stick to this glue even when it has dried completely, which certainly makes it easier to handle.

Skinner Blend

You need a pasta machine for this trick. Cut triangles from sheets of two colors of clay and fit them next to each other. Run them through the pasta machine many times, and always fold the sheet from bottom to top between each pass through the machine. The colors will blend smoothly from one to another, and you can use this blended sheet to add some extra piz-zazz to your projects.

Caneworking

Basically, a polymer clay cane is a tube or log of clay that, when assembled just right, has the same image running all the way through it when you slice it. Caneworking is a popular and easy way to add decoration to your projects. You can buy pre-made canes, but it's much more fun to make your own.

Cane Basics

- The bigger you make the cane, the more slices you get.

- Canes can be square, triangular, round, or even irregularly shaped.

- When building a cane, make sure to use the same brand of clay throughout. This will ensure that the clay is the same consistency, and your slices won't get distorted when you cut them.

- If you can, allow a cane to rest overnight after building it. The clay gets warm from all that squashing and rolling, and if you try to cut slices right away, they might be distorted. Another trick is to put a warm cane in the refrigerator for 30 minutes.

- To make a cane longer and smaller in diameter (called *reducing*), slowly and gently roll it back and forth with deliberate motions. To minimize distortion, make sure you reduce the cane evenly from one end to the other. (If the cane is too long to handle, cut off sections small enough to roll evenly.)

- To reduce a square cane, use a brayer to roll from the center of the cane to each end. Continue this process, and occasionally flip it over so that the direction of the pressure you're applying is even on all ends.

Jelly Roll Cane

This is a simple cane that looks great. Roll out rectangular sheets of two or more different colors of clay. Stack the sheets, gently press them together to eliminate air bubbles, and trim the edges so that they're all the same size. Turn one of the short ends of the stack upward, and roll up the stack to form a tube.

Bull's-Eye Cane

Use your hands to shape a single color of clay into a log. Roll out a sheet of a contrasting color, and cut it as wide as the log is long. Make a clean, straight cut along one edge of the sheet, and press the log gently into place along this edge. Carefully roll up the log inside the sheet. Where the edge presses into the sheet, roll it back a little, and you'll see the mark left by the edge. Slice away the excess clay at that mark, and finish rolling the log (the edges will butt together). Repeat this process to add as many rings as you like.

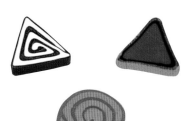

Striped Cane

Stack together two or more sheets of clay in contrasting colors. Cut the stack in half, and place one half on top of the other. Repeat this process until you have the number of stripes you want. If needed, reduce the stack by rolling the top of it with a brayer.

Checkerboard Cane

Use a rolling tool or pasta machine to roll two sheets of contrasting colors to the same thickness. Press them together gently, and trim them so that the edges are even. Cut this slab into strips, and flip over every other strip. Cut this slab in half crosswise. Stack one section on top of the other to create a checkerboard pattern.

Cutting a Cane

You've built your cane, and now it's time to cut it. The best tool for the job is the polymer clay cutting blade (page 121). To prevent smears, clean your blade with rubbing alcohol or a baby wipe cloth after every few slices. Rotate the cane a quarter turn before making your next slice,

so that you're not applying pressure to the same side, which could result in a distorted slice. If your slices are smeared, your cane may be too warm, so allow it to rest. Set the cane in the refrigerator until it's cool enough to slice cleanly.

CURING YOUR PROJECTS

No, you're not trying to make your sick polymer clay feel better. Curing or baking your clay means applying heat to your finished polymer clay project in order to make it hard. One of the great things about polymer clay is that you can bake it in the oven. According to the manufacturers, it's safe to bake in your home oven, but you should still follow some basic safety guidelines.

How to Bake

First, get a parent's permission to use the oven. Promise that you'll clean it when you're done (more on that below). Second, get an oven thermometer, and use it. Next, you need a metal tray, glass dish, or smooth ceramic tile to bake your projects on. Remember to put a piece of paper, polyester batting, or even a wadded-up piece of cotton cloth on the baking tray to avoid making a flat shiny mark on the clay.

Polymer clays bake at approximately 275°F. If the temperature is not hot enough, the polymer molecules will not fuse properly, and your finished piece will be weak. If it's too hot, your project will burn, and you'll gag on the fumes that result and send everyone out of the house until the smoke clears.

For best results, preheat the oven first using the oven thermometer as a guide.

Always refer to the polymer clay manufacturer's instructions for what temperature best suits the clay you're using. The project instructions will give you approximate times for how long to bake the clay.

Toaster Oven

You can always check the local resale shops for a toaster oven if you want to get an oven just for polymer clay. Be sure to use an oven thermometer in a toaster oven, since the oven's temperature gauge is usually inaccurate. It's also good to create a tent with aluminum foil (see photo at right) when using a toaster oven to protect your clay from the intense heat at the top of the toaster oven.

Other Oven Thoughts

- Be sure to ventilate well by keeping windows open or using the oven's exhaust fan.

- You can "tent" the baking tray you put your projects on with aluminum foil (see photo). The foil will allow the heat to cure your projects but will keep any residue from reaching the sides of the oven.

- Be sure to bake the clay for the full amount of time recommended for each project.

- While it's possible to burn the clay by baking it at too hot a temperature, it's okay to bake longer than the instructions say.

Cleaning the Oven

You can safely remove any polymer clay residue from your oven by wiping the inside of the cool oven with a little baking soda on a damp sponge, and then wiping with a wet sponge or rag. Hundreds, maybe thousands, of people bake polymer clay in their ovens and never clean them afterward; however, it can't hurt to be extra safe. If you don't have a dedicated oven, "tent" your clay or wipe down the interior as described.

DECORATING CURED PROJECTS

Just because your project is baked doesn't mean you have to be through. You can still paint your project. (Use acrylic paints.) You can also use gel pens. Use cyanoacrylate glue to stick objects to your baked projects. With this glue, ventilate well.

Squirt a little bit of glue onto wax paper, and apply it with a toothpick. And you will hardly ever glue your fingers together. And, if you want to add some shine to your finished projects, you can buy special polymer clay varnishes. Don't use nail polish! It will ruin your project.

Well, that's about it. You're ready now.

Good luck! Have fun! And return to this section if you need help!

The Projects

The best thing about polymer clay is that the more you play with it, the more comfortable you'll feel using the tools, squashing the clay, and making stuff. Sure, your first project may not look like the one in the book, but don't freak out. Working with polymer clay takes a little practice, so don't get discouraged if your first polymer clay beetle doesn't look totally awesome. Try it again. Make a bunch of beetles. Then, compare the first one to your most recent one. Not bad, eh? And if you think you've got a better way to do something, go for it. Experiment with colors, tricks, and techniques. It won't be long before you're coming up with your own project ideas.

Novel Knobs

Once you make one of these, you won't be able to stop. Your family's cabinets and dressers will never, ever be the same!

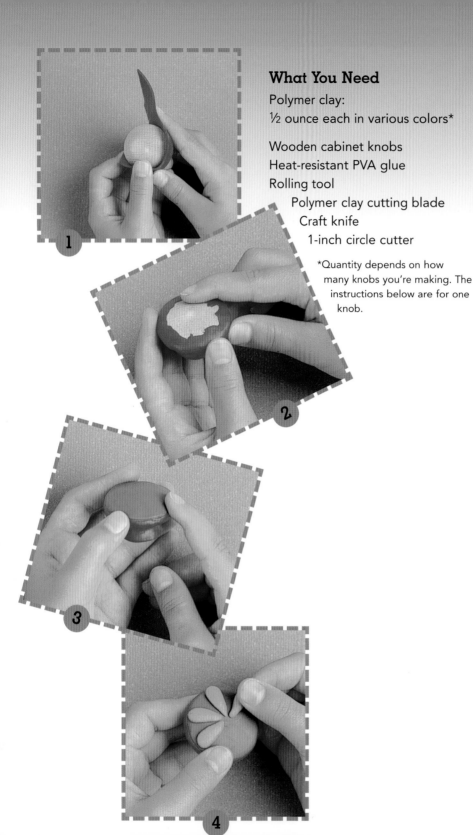

What You Need

Polymer clay:
½ ounce each in various colors*

Wooden cabinet knobs
Heat-resistant PVA glue
Rolling tool
Polymer clay cutting blade
Craft knife
1-inch circle cutter

*Quantity depends on how many knobs you're making. The instructions below are for one knob.

What You Do

1 Use your fingers to coat the cabinet knobs with a thin layer of the heat-resistant glue. Let the glue dry completely—this won't take more than 20 minutes or so.

2 Roll a sheet of clay that's long enough to wrap around the base of the knob. The clay doesn't have to cover the top of the knob—you'll decorate that later.

3 Cut one straight edge of the sheet of clay, and press it onto the side of the knob. Wrap the clay around the base of the knob, and press it to the knob as you wrap it (photo 1).

4 Trim the clay with the craft knife where it starts to over-lap, and smooth the seam with your fingertip. The top of that strip of clay you wrapped around the knob will extend partway over the edge onto the top of the knob. Smooth it with your fingers to flatten it onto the top of the knob (photo 2). Set the knob aside for a moment.

5 Roll a small sheet of clay in a contrasting color. Use the circle cutter to cut out (you guessed it) a circle. Place this on top of the knob, and press gently from the center out toward the edges to eliminate air bubbles (photo 3). This should overlap the edges of the clay you wrapped around the base of the knob.

6 Now all the interesting possibilities come in! You can roll a thin strand of another contrasting color of clay, and form a peace sign on the top of the knob. Several short, tapered snakes of clay can become flower petals (photo 4). You can use skinny snakes of clay to "draw"

on the top of the knob, or add some cane slices (see page 129). It's probably a good idea to avoid any designs that have pieces sticking out, since they might get broken off when the knobs are used. Bake the knob for 30 minutes.

Marblelous ornaments

Play with colors, shapes, textures, and sizes to create holiday decorations, gift tags, invitations, or even something for the family car's rearview mirror.

What You Need

Polymer clay:
   At least two colors that look
     nice together
Rolling tool
Texturing tools (see page 122)
Cookie cutters
Plastic drinking straw
Yarn or ribbon

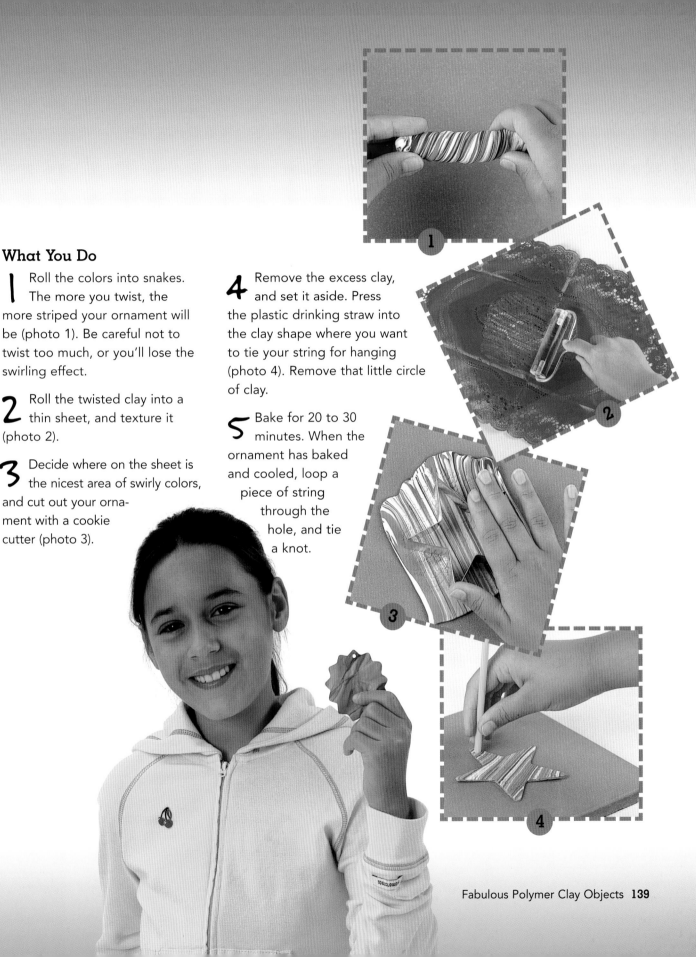

What You Do

1 Roll the colors into snakes. The more you twist, the more striped your ornament will be (photo 1). Be careful not to twist too much, or you'll lose the swirling effect.

2 Roll the twisted clay into a thin sheet, and texture it (photo 2).

3 Decide where on the sheet is the nicest area of swirly colors, and cut out your ornament with a cookie cutter (photo 3).

4 Remove the excess clay, and set it aside. Press the plastic drinking straw into the clay shape where you want to tie your string for hanging (photo 4). Remove that little circle of clay.

5 Bake for 20 to 30 minutes. When the ornament has baked and cooled, loop a piece of string through the hole, and tie a knot.

Fabulous Polymer Clay Objects **139**

Makin' Faces Switch Plates

Here are some funny faces you can make without getting in any trouble.

What You Need

Polymer clay:
- 1 ounce purple
- ½ ounce light green
- Small amounts of white, red, green, and turquoise
- Slices from a simple cane (optional)

Rolling tool

Plastic or metal light switch plate

Texturing tools (see page 122)

Craft knife

Pencil or golf tee

Brightly colored craft wire

What You Do

1 Roll out a thin sheet of purple clay. Lay it onto the front of the switch plate, and smooth from the center to the edges to work out any air bubbles. Add some texture to the clay if you want (photo 1). Flip the plate over, and trim the excess clay from the back.

2 Cut out the toggle hole in the center of the switch plate. Use the pencil or golf tee to poke the clay out of the screw holes.

3 Now's the fun—adding the face parts! (When decorating, make sure not to cover the holes you just cut out.) Cut two almond shapes from a sheet of white clay for eyes. Place these just above the toggle hole. Flatten two small balls of turquoise clay for the irises. Use a very thin strip of purple along the top edge of the eyes for eyelids (photo 2).

4 For lips, roll two marble-sized balls of red clay into short, thick logs, about 1½ inches long. Taper the ends of the logs so that each lip is much wider in the middle. Roll the edge

of a pencil along the center of one lip to create the indentation in the middle of the upper lip. Place the lips together as shown (photo 3), then place them onto the switch plate.

5 Coil the wire around the pencil. Slide it off, and spread the coils out by pulling on each end slightly. Cut this into three or more pieces. Straighten ½ inch of one end of each coil, and press this end into the switch plate on the upper edge (see photo 4 on page 142).

6 Roll a sheet of green clay, and cut it into a lop-sided rectangle for a hat (see photo 5). Place this at the top of the switch plate, covering where the wire is inserted. Decorate along the edge with the tip of the golf tee or needle tool. Trim the edges of the hat.

7 Add some hat decoration by cutting some leaf shapes from green polymer clay. Use some cane slices to represent dangling earrings, too (photo 5). Bake for 20 minutes.

Witch's Cauldron

You can cook up countless variations of this simple pot—perfect for paper clips, knick-knacks, earrings, etc. But not lizards.

What You Need

Polymer clay:
   3 ounces fuchsia
   1 ounce each of yellow
      and green
Jar lid or other flat object
Large and small star cutters
Cyanoacrylate glue

What You Do

1 Roll a 2-ounce piece of fuchsia clay into a smooth, round ball. Poke your thumb into it, and stop about halfway down. Hold the clay in one hand, and put the thumb of your other hand inside the hole. Gently enlarge the hole by pressing the clay between your thumbs and fingers, and let the sides stay curved inward toward the top (photo 1).

2 The bottom and sides will become thinner as you enlarge the hole. Work slowly and patiently for best results. If the bowl becomes too lopsided or thin, you can roll the clay back into a ball and start over. Set it aside when you're done.

3 To make the feet, roll three marble-sized balls of fuchsia, and place them about 1 inch apart. Press down on all three balls at the same time with the jar lid to flatten them (photo 2). The balls should squish toward each other and touch in the middle.

4 Center the bottom of the pot on top of the three feet, and press from the inside of the pot to make sure the feet stick (photo 3).

5 Roll the yellow clay into a thin sheet. Cut seven stars with the small cookie cutter, and place them evenly around the widest part of the pinch pot. Roll seven tiny balls of green clay, and put one in the middle of each star (photo 4). Bake the pot for 30 minutes.

6 Roll the remaining green clay into a smooth ball, and use the jar lid to press the clay into a flat disk that's larger than the opening on the pinch pot.

7 Hold the cooled pinch pot upside down, and press its opening onto the green disk (photo 5). Rotate the pinch pot a bit to leave a slight indentation in the green clay, and remove the pot. This indentation will help the lid fit perfectly on the pot.

8 Turn the lid over, cut a large star from the remaining yellow clay, and center it on the green disk.

9 Roll the remaining fuchsia clay into a long cone shape with a pointy end (photo 6). Press the bottom of the cone in the middle of the yellow star, and curl the pointy end. Bake the lid for 30 minutes.

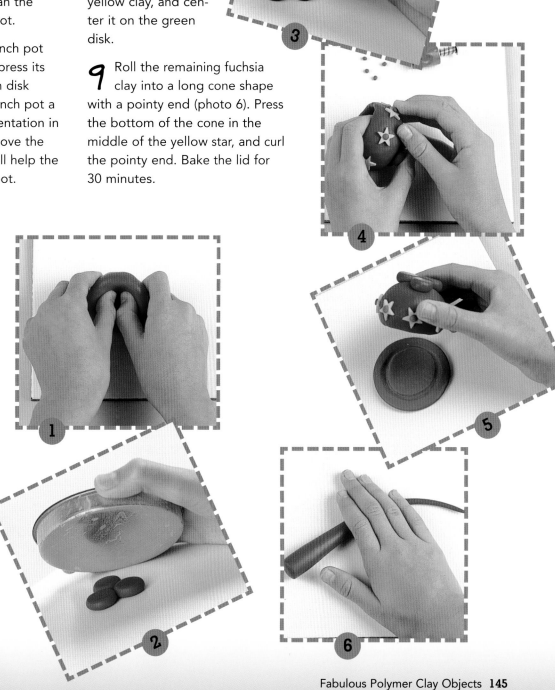

Doughnut Designs

Now presenting: the incredible, inedible doughnut pendant.

What You Need

Polymer clay:
  Black-and-white jelly roll cane
    (see page 129), ½ inch in
    diameter
  1 ounce fuchsia
Polymer clay cutting blade
Bamboo skewer
Fat knitting needle
3 feet of 1 mm black rubber or
  leather cord

What You Do

1 Squeeze the black-and-white jelly roll cane into a triangle (photo 1). Cut off 2 inches of the cane, and set it aside. Gently pull and squeeze the remaining cane, keeping the triangular shape, until it is about ¼ inch high. Set it aside.

2 Roll the fuchsia clay into a smooth, seamless ball. Hold the ball between the palms of your hands, and press your palms together gently to flatten the ball into a thick disk.

3 Use the skewer to poke a hole through the center of the disk. Turn the disk over, and poke the skewer back through the hole, using a circular motion to enlarge the hole. When the hole is large enough, insert the knitting needle, still using the circular motion to enlarge the hole until it's about ½ inch in diameter (photo 2). The disk should now look like a doughnut.

4 With the cutting blade, cut seven slices from the large triangle cane and 14 slices from the smaller cane. Position the slices in three circular rows as shown in photo 3. If you place the slices very lightly on the doughnut, you'll be able to pick them up and reposition them so they're evenly spaced around the hole.

5 When the slices are positioned the way you want them, press lightly on each slice to stick it onto the doughnut. Don't mash them; just press enough so they stick. Bake for 30 minutes. When the project is cool, thread and knot the rubber or leather cord through the hole.

Pushpinzzzzzzzz

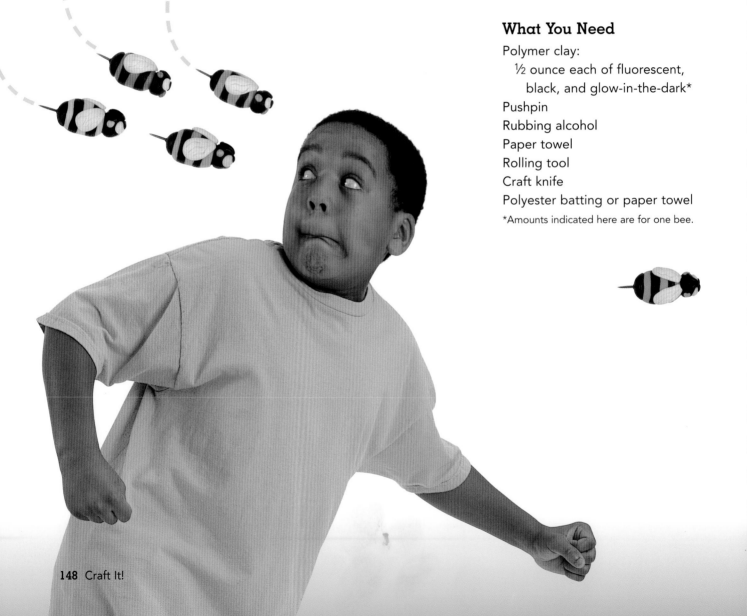

People are sure to buzz around your bulletin board if you make and use these bee-utiful pushpins.

What You Need

Polymer clay:
  ½ ounce each of fluorescent, black, and glow-in-the-dark*
Pushpin
Rubbing alcohol
Paper towel
Rolling tool
Craft knife
Polyester batting or paper towel

*Amounts indicated here are for one bee.

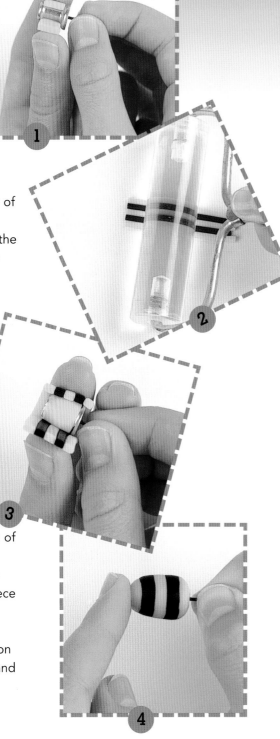

What You Do

1 Clean one pushpin with a little bit of rubbing alcohol on a paper towel. Roll the fluorescent clay into a ¼-inch-thick sheet. Cut a strip from this sheet wide enough to fill in the middle area of the pushpin. Place the clay around the middle of the pin, and press it into place (photo 1). Trim with the craft knife so that the clay doesn't overlap. Set this aside.

2 Roll some thin spaghetti-sized snakes, some in the same fluorescent color you used to cover the pushpin, and some in black. Cut them into pieces about as long as your index finger.

3 Line the snakes up, alternating black and fluorescent, until you have a strip about ½ inch wide. Gently flatten them slightly with the rolling tool until they stick to each other (photo 2).

4 Trim the strip until it's as wide as the body of the pushpin. Cut one edge straight. Place it onto the body of the pushpin, and roll it so the stripes go around the body all the way without overlapping. Press the stripes in place (photo 3).

5 Very gently smooth the seam. Don't worry if you can't make it perfectly smooth—you can put the wings there later to cover it. With your fingers, round off the top and bottom to make the body into an egg shape (photo 4).

6 To finish the body, roll a piece of black clay into a ball the size of a pea. Cut it in half. Insert the point of the stinger, I mean the pin, into the flat side of one piece of the black clay, and push the clay up the pin until it touches the striped body (see photo 5 on page 150). Press it to adhere, and smooth where you need to.

7 Use the other half of the pea-sized ball you made in step 6, and roll it into a ball for the head. Stick it to the body (photo 6). Use glow-in-the-dark and black clay to make eyes, a mouth, and antennae.

8 Roll two pea-sized, glow-in-the-dark teardrop shapes for the wings. Flatten them slightly, and press them onto the body. Bake the bee on a piece of polyester batting or wadded paper towel for 30 minutes. For more bees, simply use different colors of clay.

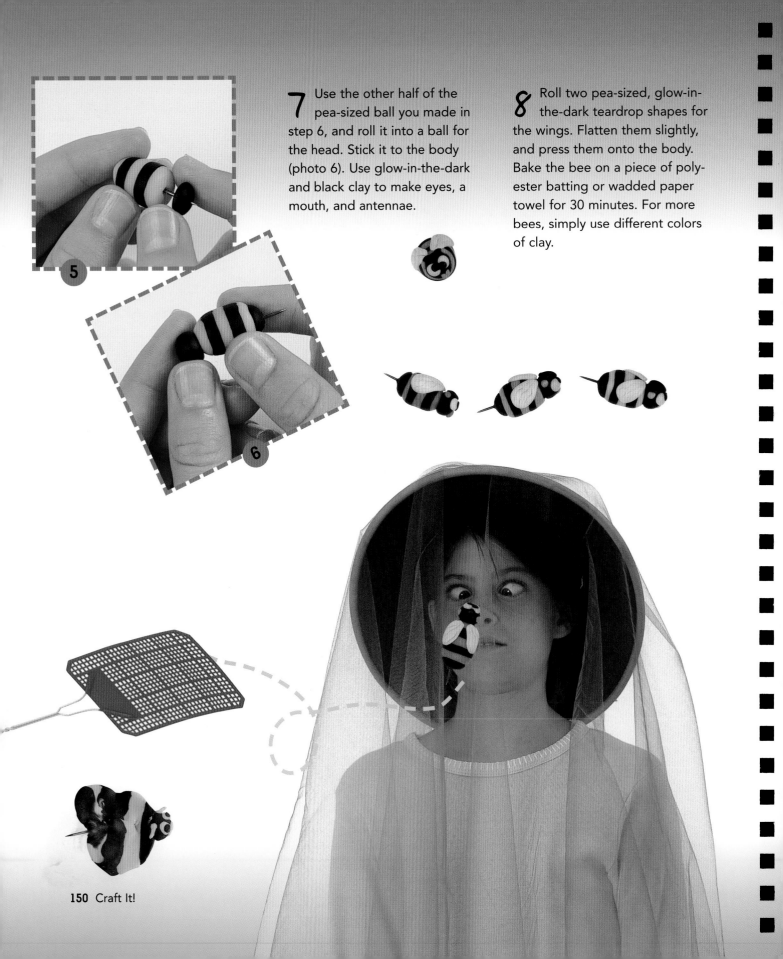

Window Clings

Liquid polymer clay is a cool material that's just what it sounds like. Window Clings are also just what they sound like. Also very cool.

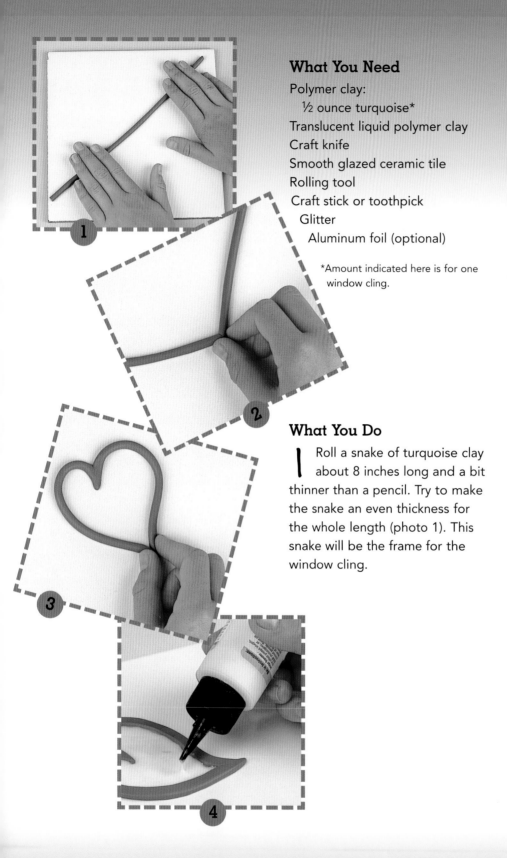

What You Need

Polymer clay:
    ½ ounce turquoise*
Translucent liquid polymer clay
Craft knife
Smooth glazed ceramic tile
Rolling tool
Craft stick or toothpick
    Glitter
    Aluminum foil (optional)

*Amount indicated here is for one window cling.

What You Do

1 Roll a snake of turquoise clay about 8 inches long and a bit thinner than a pencil. Try to make the snake an even thickness for the whole length (photo 1). This snake will be the frame for the window cling.

2 Cut the snake into two equal-sized pieces. Slice each end of both snakes at an angle. Join the ends together as shown in photo 2, and lightly smooth the seam. This is the center point of the heart. Gently press the center point down onto the ceramic tile just enough to hold it in place.

3 Form the snake pieces into the heart shape, and pinch and smooth the clay together (photo 3). Roll over the frame ever so slightly. You just want the frame to stick completely to the tile; you don't want to squish it flat.

4 Squeeze a small amount of the liquid clay inside the heart along the frame's edge, and then add a small amount in the center. Just use enough liquid clay to fill the inside area of the heart (photo 4). Be careful not to go over the edges.

5 Use the craft stick or toothpick to move the liquid clay slowly around until the inside area is completely filled in and touching all sides of the clay. Let this sit for 15 minutes so it will level out.

6 Sprinkle a tiny pinch of glitter onto the top of the liquid clay (photo 5). Don't stir the liquid clay, no matter how tempting it seems. Add glitter to the frame as well (photo 6).

7 Time to bake! When you carry the tile to the oven, be sure to keep it flat so the liquid clay won't run over the edges of the frame. Bake in a preheated oven for 15 minutes at the manufacturer's recommended temperature. Liquid polymer clay is pretty stinky when baking, so make a tent with aluminum foil, as shown on page 131, and make sure you open a window. After 15 minutes, shut the oven off, and leave the tile in the oven to cool for an hour.

8 When cool, peel the cling from the tile slowly. Your cling can now be pressed to a clean window or mirror!

LIQUID POLYMER CLAY

- Comes in white and translucent, but you can color it by stirring in a drop or two of oil paint.

- Can be used as a glue to stick two pieces of clay together. Even if the two pieces of clay have been baked, you have to bake them again so the liquid clay hardens.

- Creates a very noticeable odor when it's baking. Be sure to ventilate well!

- Can be dribbled, brushed, or smeared on a project to add decoration.

It's a Holdup

...for favorite photos, messages, and notes, that is. Make your holder as big or small as you want, and decorate it to your heart's content.

What You Need

Polymer clay:
  2 ounces pale blue
  Less than ½ ounce each of
    pink, purple, green, yellow,
    and black
Rolling tool
Coarse sandpaper or
  kitchen scrubbing pad
Craft knife
Templates on page 171
16- or 18-gauge craft wire
  (for holders)
22- or 24-gauge craft wire
  (optional)
Wire cutters
Small pliers
Ruler
Cyanoacrylate glue
Assorted beads (optional)

What You Do

1 To make the base, roll the pale blue clay into a ball, and then flatten the bottom to create a dome. Texture it with the sandpaper or scrubbing pad (photo 1).

2 Flatten the yellow, pink, and purple clay into ⅛-inch-thick sheets.

3 Use the templates on page 171 to cut out the shapes to decorate the base. Press the shapes firmly to the base. Then roll some small pieces of black for the butterfly bodies, and place them on the wings (photo 2).

4 For the grass, roll green clay into a thin sheet, and cut it into small strips. Then cut tiny slits in these strips with your craft knife. Gently separate these "blades" when pressing the strips to the base (photo 3).

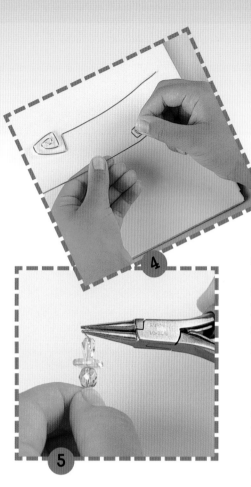

5 Use a piece of wire to poke holes in the top of the base where you plan to add "holders" later. Make sure the holes are about ½ inch deep. Bake the base for at least 20 minutes.

6 While that's baking, cut a 10-inch piece of craft wire for each hole you made in the base. Use the pliers to curl one end of each wire into a small, simple shape. Hold this part between your thumb and index finger, and continue curling into a spiral, following the same shape and enlarging as you go around, as shown in photo 4. You should bend the wire around at least three times to make an effective holder.

7 When you've made it the size you want, bend the rest of the wire away from the shape at a 90° angle. Insert the wires into the baked and cooled base, checking for length. Remove the wire, and trim the excess, if there is any.

8 Apply the glue to the end of each wire, and reinsert it into the holes on the base.

9 Want to add some dangles? Cut the thinner wire into short lengths. Curl one end into a small spiral or zigzag shape, and add some beads. Trim all but ¼ inch of the wire, and use your pliers to turn it into a loop. Open the loop slightly to add the bead to the wire holder, and then squeeze closed gently with the pliers (photo 5).

Accordion Book

This book can be a mini-journal, a card
for a friend, or simply a place for your
doodlings, random ideas, or plans to change
the world. Your choice.

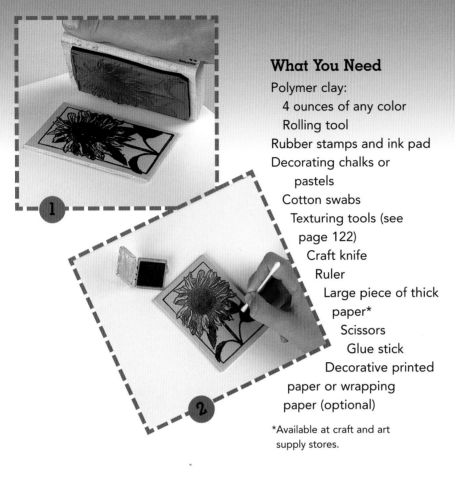

What You Need

Polymer clay:
  4 ounces of any color
  Rolling tool
Rubber stamps and ink pad
Decorating chalks or
    pastels
Cotton swabs
  Texturing tools (see
    page 122)
    Craft knife
    Ruler
    Large piece of thick
      paper*
      Scissors
      Glue stick
    Decorative printed
paper or wrapping
paper (optional)

*Available at craft and art
  supply stores.

What You Do

1 Decide how big you want
  your book to be. Roll a sheet
of clay about 1/8 inch thick, and
cut it to the size you want the
cover to be.

2 For the front cover, ink the
  rubber stamp, and stamp the
image into the center of the polymer clay sheet. Press firmly, but
not so hard that the stamp
squashes into the clay (photo 1).

3 Once the ink is completely
  dry (you may have to bake
the cover for five minutes), rub a
cotton swab on one of the chalks
or pastels to pick up the color,
and gently rub it onto the
stamped image (photo 2). Use a
different swab for each color.

4 For the back cover, texture the other sheet of clay with interesting objects or rubber stamps. Cut it to the same size as the front cover. Bake them both for 30 minutes, and let them cool.

5 Cut a long strip from your sheet of large paper, ½ inch smaller (in height) than the clay covers. Fold the strip of paper back and forth accordion-style (like you're making a paper fan), making it just a little less wide than the book covers (photo 3). If there's a little extra at the end, cut it off. Crease the folds by running your fingernail over each one.

6 To attach the paper to the covers, run the glue stick over one of the end pages, and press the paper firmly to the inside of the clay cover (photo 4). Repeat with the back cover.

7 If you'd like decorative endpapers in your book, cut two pieces of pretty paper a little smaller than the book covers and a little larger than the pages glued into the ends of the book. Glue these decorative paper sheets over the first and last pages (photo 5).

Space Mobile

Intergalactic! Cosmic!
Out of this world!

What You Need

Polymer clay:
  4 ounces glow-in-the-dark
  Small amount of silver
Star, moon, etc. cookie cutters or
  templates on page 172
Rolling tool
Needle tool
6-inch wood or plastic embroidery
  hoop*
Lightweight fishing line or black
  sewing thread
Tape measure
Tape
Glue
Small "S" hook for hanging mobile**

*Available at craft stores
**Available at home improvement centers

What You Do

1 Roll out the glow-in-the-dark clay into a sheet about ⅛ inch thick.

2 Make the celestial objects by cutting out six shapes with the cookie cutters. You can use the templates on page 172 as well. Decorate the shapes with small pieces of silver polymer clay, as shown in photo 1.

3 Poke a small hole in the top of each shape with the needle tool. Bake the shapes for 20 minutes. Glow-in-the-dark clay can sometimes burn easily, so use an aluminum foil tent over the baking tray (see page 131).

4 To make the hanger for the mobile, cut three pieces of fishing line or thread, each about 12 inches long. Tie them onto the hoop so they're spaced evenly around it. Bring the three ends together, and tie a knot (photo 2).

5 Once the shapes are cooled, tape a 2-foot length of fishing line to each one (photo 3). Determine which two shapes are the heaviest, and tie them to the hoop opposite each other. Tie the rest of the shapes onto the hoop at varying heights. Try to space them evenly apart.

6 Put the "S" hook in the loop you made in step 4. Ask an assistant to hold the mobile up in the air. Move the shapes up or down on their strings until the mobile is balanced, and you like the range of heights. When they're where you want them, remove the tape, tie each piece to its string, and snip off the excess. Glue the strings to the embroidery hoop.

Prehistoric Pencil Cup

Get totally Neanderthal with this instant ancient artifact.

What You Need

Polymer clay:
  4 ounces light tan
  ¼ ounce black
Tan and black jelly roll cane
  (see page 129)
Red, black, and gold
  triangular bull's-eye cane
  (see pages 129 and 147)
Jar
Rolling tool
Toothpick
Coarse sandpaper
Brown or burnt umber
  acrylic paint
Paper towels

What You Do

1 Find the perfect pencil-cup-sized jar, and wash and dry it thoroughly. Roll out a sheet of light tan clay. Wrap it around the jar, pressing from the middle outward to eliminate any air bubbles. Leave the edges very ragged to enhance that just-excavated look. Be sure to cover the bottom of the jar, too, and wrap the clay just slightly over the lip of the jar (photo 1).

2 Make the jelly roll cane (see page 129), using some of the same tan clay rolled up in black. Cut a few thin slices, lay them onto the jar, and roll them into the background (photo 2).

3 Use the toothpick to etch images into the clay. Hold the jar cupped gently in one hand, and etch with the other. Don't push the toothpick all the way through to the jar; just scratch the images onto the surface (photo 3). If you make a mistake, smooth the clay with your thumb and start again.

4 Texture the clay with sandpaper just a little in random places. You can also make some nicks and scratches in the clay if you haven't made enough already.

5 Apply some slices of a cane around the rim of the jar (photo 4). (This project uses a triangular bull's-eye cane—see page 147). Bake the clay-covered jar for 30 minutes. Allow it to cool completely.

6 With your fingers, spread brown or burnt umber acrylic paint onto the jar, in small sections (photo 5). When you've painted one section, rub the extra paint off with a paper towel (photo 6). Continue until you've painted and wiped the entire surface. If the paint dries before you can wipe it off, wet it with a drop or two of water and rewipe.

Beetlemania

Make 'em, name 'em, and give 'em a home on your refrigerator, school locker, desk, or any other metallic surface. Don't worry: they're not picky.

What You Need

Polymer clay:
   Fun colors of scrap clay
   ¼ ounce black
Polymer clay cutting blade
Rolling tool
1½-inch circle cookie cutter
Circle cutters in various sizes
Needle tool
Thin craft wire in various colors
Wire cutters
Magnet
Cyanoacrylate glue

What You Do

1 Steps 1 through 6 show you how to create a cool "mirror technique." It's fun, but you can skip it if you wish, and simply create any kind of dome shape for your bug. Marble two colors of scrap clay (see page 127) (photo 1).

2 Push the ends of the snake toward each other, making it fatter and about 1½ inches long. Flatten this to make it a thick rectangle.

3 With the blade, slice through the center of the rectangle, and carefully pull the halves apart. The halves will be mirror images of each other (photo 2).

4 Lay the halves next to each other, matching up the pattern in the center. With your roller, gently flatten to a ⅛-inch thickness to unite the pieces.

5 Cut a circle from this piece using the 1½-inch circle cutter, making sure the center of the mirror image is in the center of the circle (photo 3). Set it aside.

6 Roll a small ball of scrap clay about ½ inch in diameter. With the palm of your hand, flatten it slightly to form a dome (photo 4). Drape the mirror image circle on top of the dome, and press around the edges to cover it (photo 5, page 168).

7 Use the needle tool to make a straight indentation following the center line of the mirror image. This divides the bug body in half visually.

8 Roll out a small thin sheet of clay in a color that looks nice with your bug body. Cut a circle from it. Then cut this circle in half. These half-circles are the wings. Place the wings onto the bug body, touching where the head will be and opening over the sides (photo 6).

9 Roll a ball of black clay for the head, and press it to the bug where the wings connect (photo 7).

10 For the antennae, wrap some colored wire around the needle tool many times. Slide it off, cut it in half with the wire cutters, and stretch it out a little bit. Screw a piece of wire into the bug's head on both sides (photo 8). You can also twist beads onto the wire for the ends of the antennae. Or have many different-sized wings stacked on top of each other. For further decoration, add tiny balls of clay or tiny cane slices to the wings (see page 129). Bake your bug for 30 minutes, and when cool, glue the magnet to the bottom.

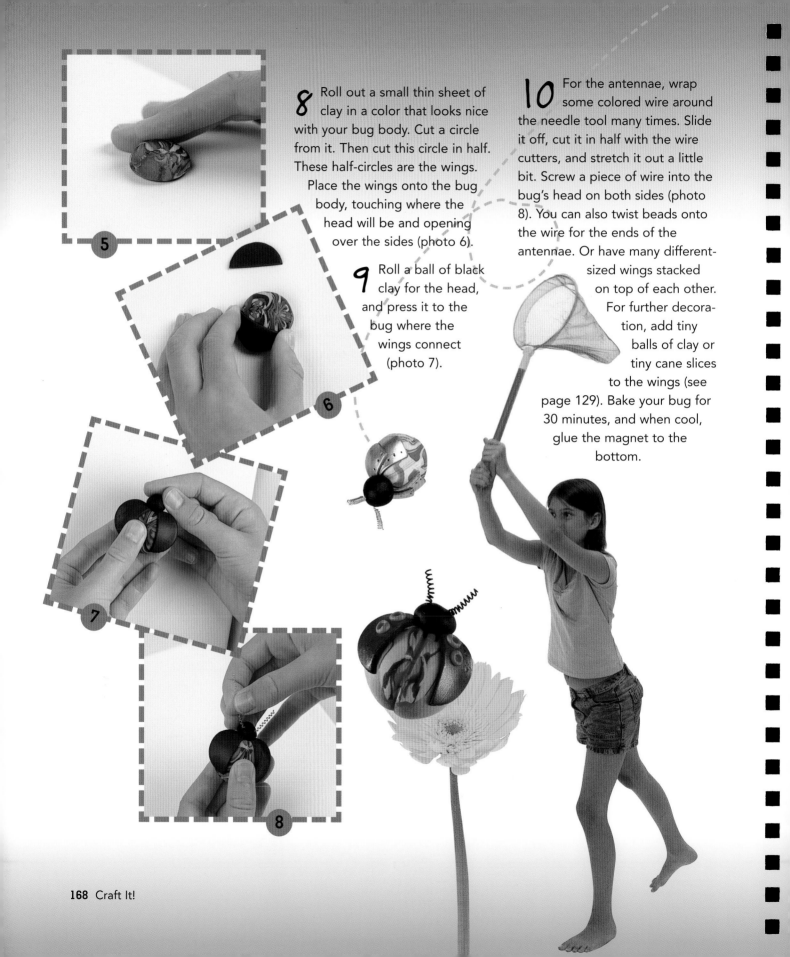

5

6

7

8

framed!

Why settle for a boring picture frame when, with a little polymer clay and some gel pens, you can create a frame that's a master-piece all by itself?

What You Need

Polymer clay:
  2 ounces black
Rolling tool
44 x 6-inch acrylic picture
  frame
Rubber stamps*
Paper towels
Heavy book
Craft knife
Assorted gel pens
Scissors
Craft glue

*All rubber-stamped images used here are
  by Impression-Obsession.

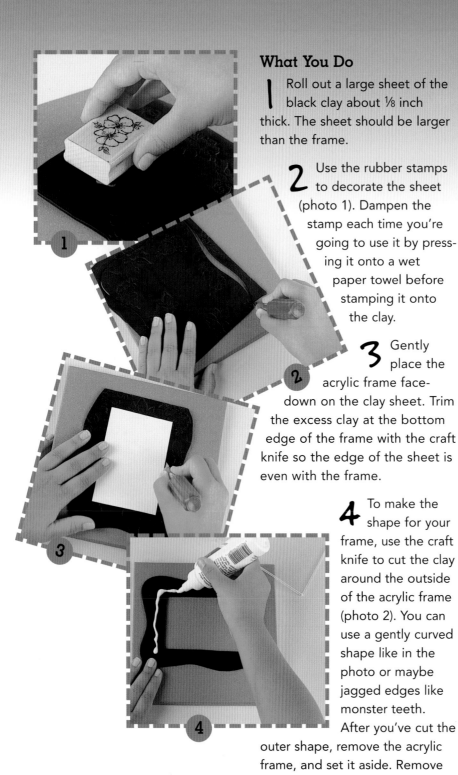

What You Do

1. Roll out a large sheet of the black clay about ⅛ inch thick. The sheet should be larger than the frame.

2. Use the rubber stamps to decorate the sheet (photo 1). Dampen the stamp each time you're going to use it by pressing it onto a wet paper towel before stamping it onto the clay.

3. Gently place the acrylic frame face-down on the clay sheet. Trim the excess clay at the bottom edge of the frame with the craft knife so the edge of the sheet is even with the frame.

4. To make the shape for your frame, use the craft knife to cut the clay around the outside of the acrylic frame (photo 2). You can use a gently curved shape like in the photo or maybe jagged edges like monster teeth. After you've cut the outer shape, remove the acrylic frame, and set it aside. Remove the excess clay from the outside of the shape you designed.

5. Cut a piece of scrap paper to the size and shape you want for the frame opening (where the photograph will go). Center it on the clay, and cut the clay around the paper (photo 3). Remove the excess clay.

6. Smooth any edges that need it, and bake for 20 minutes.

7. When the frame has finished baking, remove it from the oven while it's still warm, and put it on a flat surface. Set your heaviest science book on top of it so it remains flat as it cools. A math book will also work.

8. When the frame has cooled completely (it should take about 30 minutes), use gel pens to color the stamped areas of the frame. Not all gel pens show up on dark clay, so experiment to see which ones give you the best results.

9. After you've colored the frame with the gel pens, put the frame back in the oven at about 250°F for 10 to 15 minutes. This sets the gel inks so they won't rub off. When it's cooled off again, use the craft glue to attach the clay to the acrylic frame (photo 4).

Templates

- - - - - - - - - - - - - - - - - - - -

3-D Birthday Greetings, page 104

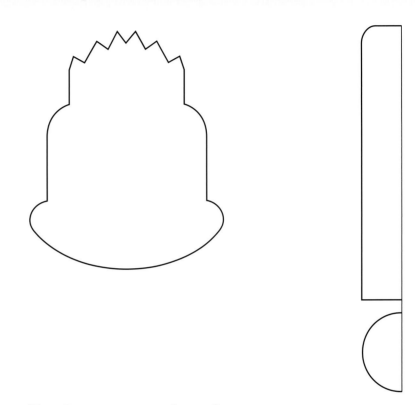

Use these two templates for the butterfly wings on It's a Holdup on page 154

Use these templates for the Space Mobile on page 160

Metric Chart

Inches	Centimeters	Inches	Centimeters
$1/8$	3 mm	12	30
$1/4$	6 mm	13	32.5
$3/8$	9 mm	14	35
$1/2$	1.3	15	37.5
$5/8$	1.6	16	40
$3/4$	1.9	17	42.5
$7/8$	2.2	18	45
1	2.5	19	47.5
$1 1/4$	3.1	20	50
$1 1/2$	3.8	21	52.5
$1 3/4$	4.4	22	55
2	5	23	57.5
$2 1/2$	6.25	24	60
3	7.5	25	62.5
$3 1/2$	8.8	26	65
4	10	27	67.5
$4 1/2$	11.3	28	70
5	12.5	29	72.5
$5 1/2$	13.8	30	75
6	15	31	77.5
7	17.5	32	80
8	20	33	82.5
9	22.5	34	85
10	25	35	87.5
11	27.5	36	90

Multiply ounces by 28 to get grams. Subtract 32 from Fahrenheit temperatures, and then multiply by .56 to get degrees in Celsius.

Acknowledgments

Thanks to our wonderful models: **Chance Barry, Karlie Budge, Aja Cobbs, Betty Cobbs, Jasmine Sky Figlow, Summer Griffin, Chloe Heimer, Natalie Anne Hopkins, Boone Kaeck, Jacob Katz, Dorothy Kaeck, Shirah Lee, Sarah Levinson, Elizabeth Lineback, Andy Massey, Maggie Mathena, Corrina Matthews, Olivia Patterson, Isaac Paul, Dylan Peifer, Natasha Perez, Niroshka Perez, JJ Peterson, Jazzman Peterson, Ray Ray Peterson, Candace Richardson, Moriah Sky Rullmoss, Leila Scogin, Alexandra Stromberg, Alexander Villarreal, Jasmine Villarreal, Jerita Villarreal, Tobie Grace Weshner, Anna Weshner-Dunning, Chelsea Pryor Wise, Kayla Wolhart, Dylan Wolhart, John Zimmerman, Lila Zimmerman, and Sebastian** (woof!).

Thanks to the big kids at heart who made the projects in this book:

Jenny Begingue (Witch's Cauldron, Doughnut Designs)
Irene Semanchuk Dean (Novel Knobs, Marbleous Ornaments, Makin'-Faces Switch Plates, Prehistoric Pencil Cup)
Dietra Garden (Flower Power Cards, Add Pizzazz to Your Scrapbooks)
Georgana Gersabeck (Pushpinzzzzzzzz, Window Clings)
Marilyn Hastings (Garland, Holiday Heart Box, Paper Bouquet, Animal Print Box)
Debbie Kreuger (Beetlemania)
Lynn Krucke (Sun Card, It's a Holdup, Framed!)
Marthe Le Van (Sunny Citrus Picture Frame)
Diana Light (Bug Frames)
Ambra Lowenstein (Place Mat)
Joan Morris (Giant Duffel Bag, Dog Bowl and Mat, Bookmark, Too Cool Bandannas, Sunflower Lampshade, Paper Bag Book Cover)
Gerri Newfry (Accordion Book)
Terry Taylor (Simply Divine Sneakers, Big Birthday Platter, Pet Silhouettes)
Kathryn Temple (Hand Towel, Orizomegami Clipboard, Dream Travel Box, Book Necklace, Interlocking Paper Bracelet)
Karen Timm (3-D Birthday Greetings, The Amazing Enveletter, Wrinkly Gift Wrap)
Luann Udell (Stationery Set)
Amy Van Aarle (Starlight Gift Wrap, Nature Calendar, Garden Party, Shake-It-Up Journal, Sponge-Painted Photo Album, Paper-Filled Ornaments)
Diane Villano (Space Mobile)

Where to Buy Supplies

Usually, the supplies you need for making the projects can be found at your local craft supply store, discount mart, home improvement center, or retail shop relevant to the topic of the book. Occasionally, however, you may need to buy materials or tools from specialty suppliers. In order to provide you with the most up-to-date information, we have created a listing of suppliers on our Web site, which we update on a regular basis. Visit us at www.larkbooks.com, click on "Craft Supply Sources," and then click on the relevant topic. You will find numerous companies listed with their Web address and/or mailing address and phone number.

Index